Writing the Critical Essay

DRUG ABUSE

An OPPOSING VIEWPOINTS® Guide

Lauri S. Friedman, *Book Editor*

Christine Nasso, *Publisher*
Elizabeth Des Chenes, *Managing Editor*

OPPOSING
VIEWPOINTS®
SERIES

GREENHAVEN PRESS
A part of Gale, Cengage Learning

GALE
CENGAGE Learning·

Detroit • New York • San Francisco • New Haven, Conn • Waterville, Maine • London

© 2008 Gale, a part of Cengage Learning

For more information, contact
Greenhaven Press
27500 Drake Rd.
Farmington Hills, MI 48331-3535
Or you can visit our Internet site at gale.cengage.com

Articles in Greenhaven Press anthologies are often edited for length to meet page requirements. In addition, original titles of these works are changed to clearly present the main thesis and to explicitly indicate the author's opinion. Every effort is made to ensure that Greenhaven Press accurately reflects the original intent of the authors. Every effort has been made to trace the owners of copyrighted material.

LIBRARY OF CONGRESS CATALOGING-IN-PUBLICATION DATA

Drug abuse / Lauri S. Friedman, book editor.
  p. cm. — (Writing the critical essay)
  Includes bibliographical references and index.
  ISBN-13: 978-0-7377-3461-4 (hardcover)
  1. Drug abuse. 2. Drug abuse--Prevention. 3. Essay--Authorship. I. Friedman, Lauri S.
  HV5801.D594 2008
  362.29—dc22

2007030799

ISBN-10: 0-7377-3461-4 (hardcover)

Printed in the United States of America
2 3 4 5 6 7 12 11 10 09 08

CONTENTS

E xamining the state of writing and how it is taught in the United States was the official purpose of the National Commission on Writing in America's Schools and Colleges. The commission, made up of teachers, school administrators, business leaders, and college and university presidents, released its first report in 2003. "Despite the best efforts of many educators," commissioners argued, "writing has not received the full attention it deserves." Among the findings of the commission was that most fourth-grade students spent less than three hours a week writing, that three-quarters of high school seniors never receive a writing assignment in their history or social studies classes, and that more than 50 percent of first-year students in college have problems writing error-free papers. The commission called for a "cultural sea change" that would increase the emphasis on writing for both elementary and secondary schools. These conclusions have made some educators realize that writing must be emphasized in the curriculum. As colleges are demanding an ever-higher level of writing proficiency from incoming students, schools must respond by making students more competent writers. In response to these concerns, the SAT, an influential standardized test used for college admissions, required an essay for the first time in 2005.

Books in the Writing the Critical Essay: An Opposing Viewpoints Guide series use the patented Opposing Viewpoints format to help students learn to organize ideas and arguments and to write essays using common critical writing techniques. Each book in the series focuses on a particular type of essay writing—including expository, persuasive, descriptive, and narrative—that students learn while being taught both the five-paragraph essay as well as longer pieces of writing that have an opinionated focus. These guides include everything necessary to help students research, outline, draft, edit, and ultimately write successful essays across the curriculum, including essays for the SAT.

Using Opposing Viewpoints

This series is inspired by and builds upon Greenhaven Press's acclaimed Opposing Viewpoints series. As in the parent series, each book in the Writing the Critical Essay series focuses on a timely and controversial social issue that provides lots of opportunities for creating thought-provoking essays. The first section of each volume begins with a brief introductory essay that provides context for the opposing viewpoints that follow. These articles are chosen for their accessibility and clearly stated views. The thesis of each article is made explicit in the article's title and is accentuated by its pairing with an opposing or alternative view. These essays are both models of persuasive writing techniques and valuable research material that students can mine to write their own informed essays. Guided reading and discussion questions help lead students to key ideas and writing techniques presented in the selections.

The second section of each book begins with a preface discussing the format of the essays and examining characteristics of the featured essay type. Model five-paragraph and longer essays then demonstrate that essay type. The essays are annotated so that key writing elements and techniques are pointed out to the student. Sequential, step-by-step exercises help students construct and refine thesis statements; organize material into outlines; analyze and try out writing techniques; write transitions, introductions, and conclusions; and incorporate quotations and other researched material. Ultimately, students construct their own compositions using the designated essay type.

The third section of each volume provides additional research material and writing prompts to help the student. Additional facts about the topic of the book serve as a convenient source of supporting material for essays. Other features help students go beyond the book for their research. Like other Greenhaven Press books, each book in the Writing the Critical Essay series includes bibliographic listings of relevant periodical articles, books, Web sites, and organizations to contact.

Writing the Critical Essay: An Opposing Viewpoints Guide will help students master essay techniques that can be used in any discipline.

Strategies for Reducing Drug Abuse in America

Drug abuse continues to be a problem in the United States, despite more than half a century of efforts to eradicate the problem. Contrary to what some believe, drug abuse is not just a personal problem; it is a cause of serious social problems that affect all Americans, such as poverty, crime, homelessness, and domestic violence, and contributes to the spread of diseases such as hepatitis, HIV, and AIDS. Although American politicians, lawmakers, social workers, and others have been considering solutions to this problem for decades, disagreement continues to exist over how to reduce drug abuse and the societal problems it causes. Two different strategies are usually considered when people discuss ways to solve the problems caused by drug abuse: "harm reduction" and "zero-tolerance". Understanding the differences between these two drug abuse reduction strategies is an important part of studying drug abuse.

Those who subscribe to the harm reduction strategy operate under the assumption that some people will always use drugs despite society's best efforts to stop them. According to the organization DanceSafe, which works to promote a safe environment for partygoers, "despite all our efforts as a society to stop the use of illicit drugs, people are using them anyway, and it seems unlikely this situation is going to change soon."[1] Organizations such as DanceSafe believe that instead of trying to harshly penalize drug users and permanently eradicate all drug use, users should be treated in ways which reduce their harm to society and themselves. Explains DanceSafe, "Harm reduction programs provide non-abstentionist health and safety information under the

---

[1] "Philosophy and Vision," DanceSafe, March 12, 2007,
  www.dancesafe.org/documents/about/philosophyandvision.php.

recognition that many people are going to choose to experiment with drugs despite all the risks involved. Harm reduction information and services help people use as safely as possible as long as they continue to use."[2] Indeed, harm reduction programs, such as needle exchanges or designated driver campaigns have saved tens of thousands of lives and prevented as many people from becoming infected with life-threatening illnesses. For these reasons, harm reduction programs are championed by supporters as a realistic, practical and humane way of helping drug users overcome their addiction and lessening the damage done to society.

There are many others, however, who believe that harm reduction policies inappropriately condone drug use. From their perspective, it is wrong to give users the impression that drug abuse in any form is acceptable. They believe the best way to eradicate drug abuse is to treat it as a serious crime that deserves punishment, a strategy known as "zero-tolerance." This strategy is dedicated to working towards a drug-free society by sending a clear, strong message that no form of drug use is to be tolerated. As Drug Watch International, a non-profit organization that promotes a drug-free society puts it: "Drug users, like any other member of society, must be held accountable for their actions. Illicit drug use must bring swift and cost effective consequences that will benefit the user and society at large."[3] Proponents of zero-tolerance believe that harm reduction policies encourage and facilitate drug use, which is counterproductive to a movement that seeks to end drug use. Advises Drug Watch International, "Every segment of society must send the message that drug use and drug use behavior will not be tolerated. Drug user accountability must be a cornerstone of national and international drug policy."[4]

[2] "Philosophy and Vision," DanceSafe, March 12, 2007, www.dancesafe.org/documents/about/philosophyandvision.php.
[3] Drug Watch Truth & Lies," Drug Watch International, July 30, 2001. www.drugwatch.org/T&L%20Drug%20User%20Accountability.htm
[4] "Drug Watch Truth & Lies," Drug Watch International, July 30, 2001. www.drugwatch.org/T&L%20Drug%20User%20Accountability.htm

Whether harm reduction policies or zero tolerance policies better solve the problem of drug abuse has yet to be determined. These strategies are just two topics that fuel the debate between politicians, social workers, psychologists, scientists, and, substance abuse counselors who seek a solution to drug abuse. What causes drug abuse, the effects it has on society, and how best to prevent it are enduring topics of study for these professionals, and many other Americans. *Writing the Critical Essay: An Opposing*

Former president Bill Clinton attends a leadership conference to discuss the problems of youth drug abuse and violence at a high school in Maryland.

LeAnn Rimes performs at a concert to celebrate the 17th Anniversary for D.A.R.E, an organization that educates children about the harms of drugs and alcohol.

Viewpoints Guide: Drug Abuse exposes readers to the basic arguments made about the causes and effects of drug abuse and helps them develop tools to craft their own essays on the subject. Through skill-building exercises and thoughtful discussion questions, students will formulate unique opinions about drug abuse and develop tools to craft their own essays on the subject.

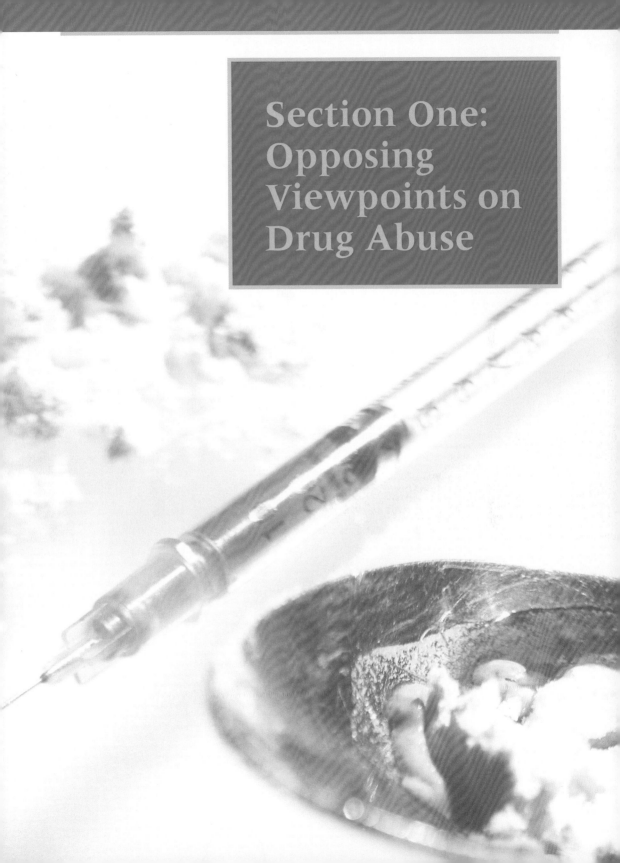

Section One:
Opposing
Viewpoints on
Drug Abuse

The War on Drugs Reduces Drug Abuse

Jonathan Last

The "War on Drugs" is a decades-old government strategy to eradicate drug supply and drug use in America. The drug war encompasses everything from anti-drug television ads to drug laws and foreign policy. In the following viewpoint, author Jonathan Last argues that the drug war has been successful. He claims that both the supply of drugs and teen drug abuse has been reduced because of it.

Last is the online editor of the conservative magazine *Weekly Standard*. He also writes a weekly editorial for the *Philadelphia Inquirer*.

Consider the Following Questions:

1. By how much has the ONDCP's budget increased since 1998, and what has this money been used to fund, according to Last?
2. Why, in the author's opinion, is so much attention given to drug-use statistics for 12- to 17-year-olds and 18- to 25-year-olds?
3. What effect has the war on drugs had on the supply of LSD, according to the author?

Jonathan Last, "We Are Winning the War on Drugs," *Philadelphia Inquirer,*
February 5, 2006, Copyright © 2006 The Philadelphia Newspapers, Inc.
Reproduced by permission.

There's a wonderful scene in the movie *Traffic* in which a captured drug kingpin, played by Miguel Ferrer, is being interrogated by two federal agents. Ferrer says to them disdainfully: "You people are like those Japanese soldiers left behind on deserted islands who think that World War II is still going on. Let me be the first to tell you, your government surrendered this war a long time ago."

It's a brilliant bit of filmmaking; it's also bunk. Over the last five years, while no one was paying attention, America has been winning its war on drugs.

Shrinking America's Drug Problem

The cosmopolitan view has long been that the fight against drugs is a losing battle; that the supply of drugs pouring into America is never-ending; that drug lords are unrelenting zombie-supermen—kill one, and five more spring up.

The American drug problem grew to epidemic proportions throughout the 1960s and 1970s. In 1979, agencies of Health and Human Services and the National Institutes of Health performed a national household survey of illicit drug use; substances included marijuana, cocaine, heroin, banned hallucinogens and inhalants, and unauthorized use of sedatives, stimulants and analgesics. As of 1979, the numbers were horrifying: 31.8 percent of teens ages 12 to 17 had used drugs; 16.3 percent of them had used in the last month. Among those ages 18 to 25 it was worse: 69 percent had used at some point; 38 percent in the last month.

But throughout the '80s, those numbers shrank. Sophisticates derided "Just Say No," [a popular anti-drug campaign of the 1980s]

> ## Winning the War on Drugs
>
> We've reduced casual use, chronic use, and prevented others from even starting. Overall drug use in the United States is down 50% since the late 1970s. ... The fact is that our current policies balancing prevention, enforcement, and treatment have kept drug usage outside the scope of acceptable behavior in the U.S.
>
> Asa Hutchison, Remarks Before the Modernizing Criminal Justice Conference, London, England, June 18, 2002.

Don't Let Your Teen's Summer Go to Pot.

but by 1993, only 16.4 percent of 12- to 17-year-olds had used, and only 5.7 percent had used in the last month. In the 18-to-25 age bracket, 50.2 percent had tried drugs, but only 15 percent had used in the last 30 days. It was a remarkable success.

Fewer Teens Use Drugs Today

From 1993 to 2001, the numbers become less rosy: Among ages 12 to 17, the percentage of youths who had tried drugs increased almost twofold. In the 18-to-25 crowd, the increase was less marked, but still noticeable.

There's a reason we pay so much attention to these two age groups. As Tom Riley, the director of public affairs at the Office of National Drug Control Policy (ONDCP), explains: "If people don't start using drugs as teenagers—the mechanism of addiction clicks much more quickly in the developing brain—then they are unlikely to ever go on to serious drug abuse. If we can reduce the number of teens who use drugs, we change the shape of the problem for generations to come."

After 2001, the tide turned again. Since then, teen drug use is off nearly 19 percent. Which means that 700,000 fewer teens are using drugs today than just a few years ago.

Cocaine Production Is Down

What happened? For one thing: funding. Since 1998, the ONDCP's real budget has increased, from $8.2 billion to $12.4 billion. That extra money has mostly gone to law enforcement and drug treatment, attacking both the supply and the demand sides of the problem. Measures for demand are fuzzy, but the supply side of the equation—the "war" part of the war on drugs—has solid metrics.

Each substance is its own front and has its own dynamics. Drug supply is shockingly local. Take coca, the substance from which cocaine and crack are derived. From 1998 to 2001, world coca production increased from 586,100 metric tons to 655,800 metric tons, with the lion's share grown in Columbia. Since then, the ONDCP orchestrated a campaign to spray 140,000 hectares of Colombian coca fields with glyphosate (you know it as Roundup). The result: world coca production is down 20 percent.

A War Worth Fighting

With other substances, the news is even better. On Nov. 6, 2000, the Drug Enforcement Agency raided an abandoned missile silo in Wamego, Kan., which housed the world's leading LSD operation. By 2004, LSD availability in America was down 95 percent. The market still hasn't recovered.

Former White House National Drug Policy Director Barry McCaffrey announces a joint federal-state partnership with Maryland to fight drug abuse in America.

The supply of all the major drugs is down, but at the same time, drug interdiction is up. In 1989, 533,533 kilograms of the four major drugs were seized by U.S. authorities. By 2005, the total had risen to 1.3 million kilograms.

Earlier this week, the ONDCP released a report outlining their order of battle for 2006. Director John Walters is not the type to go running for the nearest TV camera. Yet the quiet success he has overseen is a powerful reminder that the bad guys are not 10 feet tall; that failure is not inevitable; that the war on drugs is a war worth fighting; and that we're fighting it well.

Analyze the Essay:

1. Jonathan Last uses many facts, figures, and statistics to support his argument that the war on drugs has been successful. He does not, however, use any quotes to support his argument. Which do you think would have been a more successful tool for supporting his argument—statistics or quotes? If your answer is statistics, explain which statistics you found most persuasive. If your answer is quotes, highlight places in the text where you think quotes would have bolstered the argument.

2. The author chose to open his essay by describing a scene from a movie. Why did he do this? What does the scene illustrate, and how does the author incorporate it into his argument?

The War on Drugs Does Not Reduce Drug Abuse

Anthony Gregory

In the following viewpoint, author Anthony Gregory argues that the War on Drugs is an evil, unsuccessful war that violates the rights of Americans. Unlike crimes such as murder or theft, he contends, drug use does not harm anyone but the user. Murder and theft are illegal because they threaten peoples' right to life, liberty, happiness, and property, he explains. But drug use does not have this affect on others, and thus cannot be truly classified as a crime, reasons Gregory. Furthermore, despite millions of dollars and years of efforts, the drug war has not stopped Americans' interest in using drugs. For these reasons, Gregory concludes that the War on Drugs is a fruitless, unfair war against an act that should not be labeled as criminal.

Anthony Gregory is a writer and musician who lives in Berkeley, California. He is a research analyst at the Independent Institute, a non-profit think tank that publishes white papers and policy reports on the War on Drugs and other topics.

Consider the Following Questions:

1. According to Gregory, how many Americans have tried illegal drugs at some point in their lives?
2. In what way does the War on Drugs violate the rights of Americans, in Gregory's opinion?
3. In what way is drug use different from murder, according to the author?

Anthony Gregory, "The Drug War's Immortality and Abject Failure," LewRockwell. com, October 6, 2006. Reproduced by permission of the publisher and the author.

If the idea is to create a drug-free America, then we can safely say that after hundreds of billions of dollars spent, millions of arrests, and decades of escalating police and military efforts, the war on drugs is a complete failure. . . .

Drug Use Is Not Immoral

Proponents of continuing the war on drugs will sometimes concede its futility, but then compare their crusade to other law-enforcement endeavors with which nearly no one disagrees. They argue that even if it is impossible for the government to stop all murders, it doesn't follow that murder should be legal, and the same is true with drugs.

But comparing drug use to murder is unrealistic. The vast majority of people would agree that even if drug use is immoral in some sense, it is not immoral in the same way as murder. What many might not realize, having not been exposed to libertarian ethics, is the nature of the distinction—drug use, in and of itself, is a victimless act, whereas murder, like rape, kidnapping, assault, theft, and trespassing, is a rights violation.

Using Drugs Does Not Endanger Anyone Else

People have a right to life, liberty, and property, and to pursue happiness within the limits emerging from other people's equal rights to life, liberty, and property. If not for this, theft would not be a crime. Neither would murder nor assault. When a person is murdered, his right to life has been violated. When a person is kidnapped, his right to liberty has been infringed. When a person is robbed, his right to property has been trampled.

These criminal acts enjoy their infamy and they universally evoke emotions of anger and resentment because of the very essence of human nature and what it means to be human. Drug use, unlike any of these real crimes, does not involve a trespass against anyone's right to life, liberty, or property. On the contrary, people have a right to peacefully use drugs, and to provide drugs to those who want to obtain them by means of an honest market transaction. You may not approve of their choices, but to interfere coercively with them is itself a violent attack on their rightful liberty. . . .

There Are Too Many Drug Users to Punish

Perhaps as both a result and a cause of Americans' not seeing drug use in the same way they see crimes against person and property, tens of millions of Americans have tried illegal drugs at some time in their lives. Drug warriors need to confront this reality. Tens of millions of Americans, even if they don't use drugs now, are likely to have some sympathy for the drug offender that they don't have for the murderer or thief. While most Americans might think it would be good in theory, albeit highly improbable in the real world, to put all murderers behind bars, very few Americans would want to imprison every single person who has committed a drug crime. This is sensible, since doing so would be impossible. Even imprisoning a third of the drug offenders would be economically unfeasible. There are just too many such people. Even if you could catch them all, it would bankrupt the country to prosecute and jail them with anything resembling due process. Thus we see draconian punishments and unconstitutional law-enforcement practices employed in an effort to deter most drug users by making an example of the small minority who are caught and jailed.

This highlights a practical difference between drug users and murderers. Most of us want to see all the murderers punished. But it would destroy America to see even a substantial fraction of the drug users punished. In fact, the mere attempt to cleanse society of drugs by force has already wreaked irreparable damage on America. . . .

A Failed War

The U.S. policy of a "war on drugs" has been, is, and forever will be, a total and abject failure. This is not a war on drugs, this is a war on people—our own people— our children, our parents, ourselves.

Jack Cole, *End Prohibition Now! Law Enforcement Against Prohibition*, September 21, 2005.

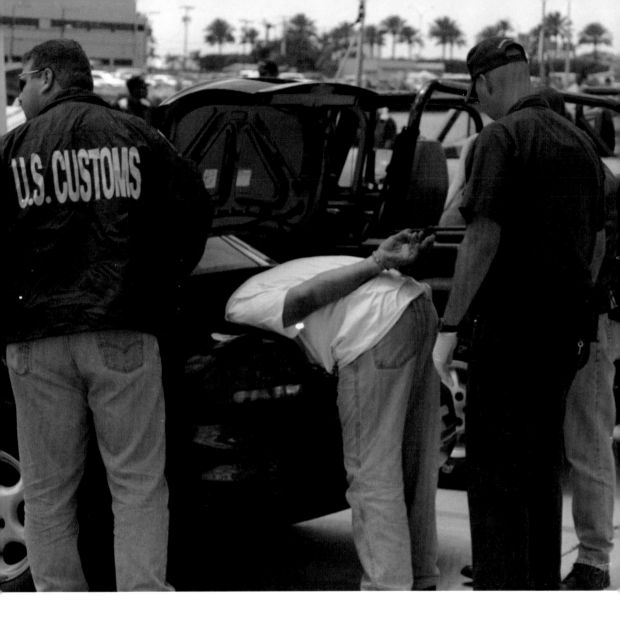

Drug Use Is Not Inherently Criminal

It is often argued that drug use must be combated because it contributes to criminal activity. Much of this is a result of the drug war, which causes drug prices to balloon, sometimes hundreds or thousands of times over, and so leads desperate addicts to steal. A lot of the crime is caused by turf wars over drug territory. Not nearly as much street crime is associated with the alcohol market now as when it was underground.

During a customs check a cocaine smuggler is caught and arrested for possession.

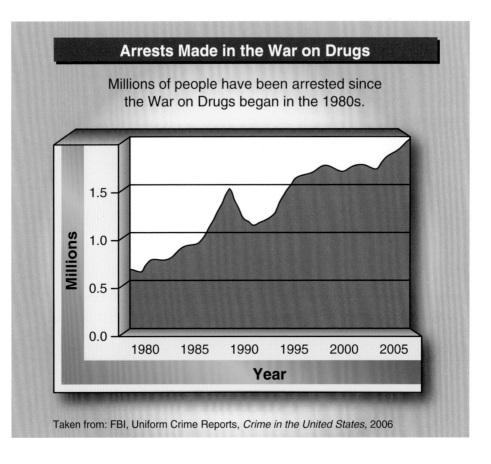

Arrests Made in the War on Drugs

Millions of people have been arrested since the War on Drugs began in the 1980s.

Taken from: FBI, Uniform Crime Reports, *Crime in the United States*, 2006

But perhaps it is true that some drugs can make some people more likely to commit crimes. It still doesn't follow that outlawing those drugs is the answer. Alcohol is in fact the leading drug associated with homicides. Making it illegal would not reduce violent crime; it would only bring back Al Capone—or, more precisely, introduce the Crips and Bloods to the liquor business. Ultimately, the principal reason that much of the drug scene is saturated by criminality is that it has been forced into the black market.

In any event, if a drug user commits a crime against person or property, he should be dealt with for that crime. It is unnecessary and in fact counterproductive and unjust to preemptively attack drug users on the basis that they might be criminals. The overwhelming majority of drug users are

nonviolent, generally law-abiding people. A significant portion of the prison system is filled with such people. Police and criminal-justice resources would be better directed against actual criminals—whether or not they use drugs. . . .

A marijuana grower from Colorado is surrounded with marijuana plants and heating lamps.

The War on Drugs Violates Rights

The drug war has subjected Americans, and foreigners as well, to a systematic abuse of their rights. Drug users are deprived of their rights to ingest what they wish, and, in many cases, are deprived of their liberty for years, never

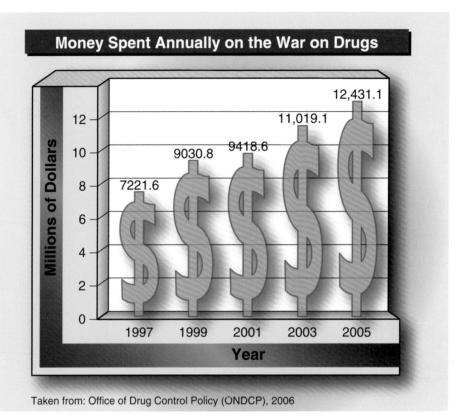

Money Spent Annually on the War on Drugs

Millions of Dollars

12,431.1

11,019.1

9418.6

9030.8

7221.6

12 — 10 — 8 — 6 — 4 — 2 — 0 —

1997   1999   2001   2003   2005

Year

Taken from: Office of Drug Control Policy (ONDCP), 2006

to get it back fully even after they're released. Non–drug users are spied on and searched in outrageous ways, all to stamp out drugs. People in need of medical marijuana suffer severely because their human right to self-medicate has been violated. . . .

No matter how much of a utopia one may think would result if drugs were eliminated, it's not going to happen, and certainly not by using government force. The laws of economics, the principles of supply, demand, and human action that undermine socialist systems, also undermine the war on drugs. Millions want to use drugs and no government program will stop them all, or even most, as long as they are willing to pay and a supplier is willing to sell. The more the state ratchets up the drug war, the higher the profits at stake, and the more innovative and determined the dealers become. Meanwhile, because of the inevitably failed drug war, America becomes more like a prison every day. . . .

An Evil and Wasteful War

Although it is a politically incorrect point, we must recognize that people have a right to put what they want into their bodies, and no one has a right to forcibly stop them. Not only does this truth flow axiomatically from any proper understanding of the human rights to life, liberty, and property; it offers the best explanation of why the drug war has been such an abject failure. Something as abjectly immoral, as contrary to human nature as the drug war cannot bring about happiness or order or civilization or progress. It can, however, effectively destroy lives and turn the country into a much worse place to live.

Americans may not think they're ready to end the drug war, but the immoral crusade is doomed to fail. The sooner we recognize this, the sooner we can begin the process of restoring the precious American freedoms that have been eroded in this very evil war.

Analyze the Essay:

1. In this viewpoint, Anthony Gregory argues that Americans have the right to use drugs if they wish because drug use does not harm anyone but the user. How do you think the author of the previous viewpoint, Jonathan Last, would respond to this claim? Use material from each author's viewpoint to support your answer.

2. After reading this viewpoint and the previous viewpoint, what is your opinion on whether the War on Drugs reduces drug use? Explain which parts of the text convinced you.

Peer Pressure Causes Drug Abuse

Jamie Gadette

In the following viewpoint, author Jamie Gadette tells the story of Eric, a Utah teenager who straggled with a devastating addiction to prescription drugs. Eric was introduced to a painkiller called OxyContin at parties and other social situations. The drug was easy to get and used by many students at his high school. Eric spent all of his money on the drug, became physical dependent on it, and isolated his family in the process. Prescription drugs have become increasingly popular with high school students, Gadette concludes, and warns that it will be hard for teens to say no to a drug that everyone else is doing.

Jamie Gadette is a staff writer for *Salt Lake City Weekly*, from which this viewpoint is taken.

Consider the Following Questions:

1. What percentage of high school students have taken prescription drugs to get high, as reported by Gadette?
2. What term does Gadette say has been given to this generation of drug users, and what does it mean?
3. From what types of families do teens who abuse prescription drugs come from, according to Gadette?

Jamie Gadette, "The Real OC," *Salt Lake City Weekly*, vol. 22, May 26, 2005, p. 22. Reproduced by permission.

OxyContin was hailed as a miracle pain reliever upon its release. Some addicts find it works a little too well.

The first time Eric tried OxyContin, he knew he was screwed. It wasn't like the other drugs he'd popped, snorted or injected after graduating from a public high school in an affluent area.

Learning About Drugs At Parties in Groups

As a teenager, Eric—who wishes to remain anonymous—managed to juggle weekend kegs with athletic and academic achievements. While his recreational use eventually expanded to include Ecstasy, cocaine and weed, partying was just a way to let loose—not a way of life. Nothing prepared him for Oxy's sucker-punch effect. In fact, the powerful prescription painkiller made all the other narcotics seem about as addictive as Fruit Loops.

"I remember thinking, 'Holy cow, it would be great if I felt like this all day, every day, for the rest of my life,'" he says. Even now, his excitement is palpable.

Today, he looks back on Oxy as a hot romance turned sour, but he'll never forget how it felt to fall—fast and hard.

It started on weekends, at parties, in a bedroom with four or five others. For a while, he'd split up one OC 20, or 20 mg of pure oxycodone, take half and save the rest for later. But his tolerance went through the roof. He needed more and more, and it was getting expensive. His group of friends started snagging OC 80 at $60 a hit. He tried stopping, but couldn't handle the withdrawals. Chills, fever, vomiting and stomach cramps wracked his body.

A Ruined Life

He worked as a garbageman, driving trucks around town, high as a kite, reflexes down. Dad and Grandma kept loaning him money, but sooner or later the gig was up.

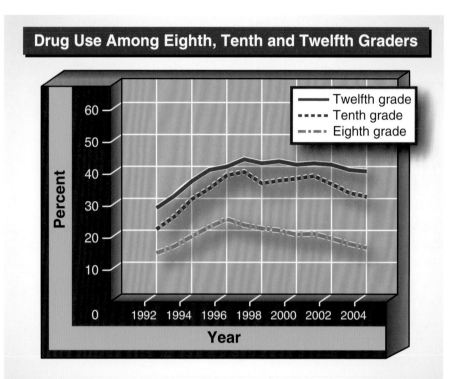

Drug Use Among Eighth, Tenth and Twelfth Graders

Twelfth grade
Tenth grade
Eighth grade

Percent

60
50
40
30
20
10
0

1992 1994 1996 1998 2000 2002 2004

Year

Taken from: "Overall teen drug use continues gradual decline, but use of inhalants rises," University of Michigan News and Information Services, December 21, 2004.

His family intervened, sent him to a pricey treatment center and called it good. Six months later, Eric quit going to Narcotics Anonymous (NA) meetings, stopped calling his sponsor and relapsed. He later tried his hand as a mail carrier, trucking through the Avenues either doped up or jonesing for drugs he no longer could easily afford. His parents cut him off. He pawned prized possessions, committed petty theft and even sold Oxy for a while. But the taste was too sweet. He wanted it all for himself. Giving Oxy up was easier once heroin stepped in. It didn't take long, however, before he had to choose between getting clean and quitting life.

That was three years ago. Today, he's eight months sober. He keeps a steady, blue-collar job, hangs out with his girlfriend and attends NA meetings every day. His drugs of choice are coffee and cigarettes. This morning, he sips a 24-ounce French roast, straight up. His shoulders are wide, cheeks full, dark hair tousled from a good night's sleep. And while his tough, football-player frame has softened, the clear-headed 25-year-old is stronger than ever. He just can't help but wonder how strong he might be today had he never tried Oxy.

Prescription Drug Abuse Is On the Rise

Eric isn't unique. Neither is OxyContin. Problem is that few experts agree on how widely it's abused. Drug counselors, law-enforcement agencies, former addicts, parents and clergy members all have a different take on the drug's societal impact. Some blame the pharmaceutical industry for marketing the drug so well. Others blame physicians too eager to prescribe it. Still others argue for an outright ban on the drug. Maybe we just need to relax, pop a pill and move on.

There's no question prescription-medication abuse is on the rise. In fact, prescribed opiate narcotics now rank second to marijuana as the nation's most-abused form of drug, according to the Substance Abuse and Mental Health Services Administration (SAMHSA). . . .

"Generation RX"

It turns out plenty of kids are unlocking Oxy's stealth impact. A recent study sponsored by the Partnership for a Drug-Free America shows prescription drug abuse is on the rise among teenagers. The report indicates approximately one in five high school students has taken prescribed opiates to get high. Eighteen percent of kids reported non-medical use of Vicodin, a slightly less addictive combination of two pain relievers, while 10 percent admitted abusing

The Need to Succeed and Belong

Missing from the picture [of teenage drug addiction] are the high-performing student athletes who do their families proud, the perfectionist fitness buffs whose internal personas become defined by their external appearance, and the little guys who know that the big guys get all of the attention and all of the dates. ... They're not taking the drugs to get high. They're taking them to get strong, to get lean, to get validation, and to get scholarships—and they're doing it under the noses of their parents, coaches, and teachers.

Diana Mahoney, "Teens and Steroids: A Dangerous Mix," *Clinical Psychiatry News*, June 2006, p. 50.

Student Steroid Use

According to the National Institute on Drug Abuse, more than a half million 8th- and 10th-graders use steroids.

	8th-Graders	10th-Graders	12th-Graders
Lifetime	1.9%	2.4%	3.4%
Annual	1.1%	1.5%	2.5%
30-day	0.5%	0.8%	1.6%

Taken from: National Institute on Drug Abuse, Monitoring the Future Survey, 2004.

Oxy. The alarming data prompted researchers to dub this new class of users, "Generation RX," a catchy term that doesn't do its subject justice.

If the slogan's true, Utah's schools could be harboring plenty of RX-ers. It's difficult to track exactly how many local students are experimenting with Oxy, considering there's little data documenting its effects across the nation, let alone in Utah. But anecdotal evidence suggests it's more popular here than scarce data indicates.

Teen Addiction Trends

Eric says his former East Bench high school exemplifies local trends. Most of the students come from wealthy LDS [Mormon] families and have regular access to well-stocked medicine cabinets. They don't pay rent, health or car insurance and, with the right ploy, can convince trusting parents to fork over cash for an innocent night at the movies. Plus, physicians tend to find insured clients' claims of injury more credible than those of inner-city patients backed by Medicare.

Culturally, Oxy isn't grouped with "dirty" street drugs like coke and heroin. Many assume that if it's legal, it's safe. After all, what's the harm in following doctor's orders? That's the sort of attitude that makes Oxy so susceptible to abuse: that, plus its invisibility. It's easier to spot a heroin addict, or at least the gear they use to shoot up. Parents who suspect their kids might be smoking pot can check bedrooms for baggies, pipes, bongs or lingering scents. Prescription medications, on the other hand, are out in the open for everyone to see—and use. All you need is a little water to swallow the tablet.

Reported Drug and Alcohol Use by High School Seniors, 2004

Drugs	Used within the last:	
	12 months	30 days
Alcohol	70.6%	48.0%
Marijuana	34.3%	19.9%
Stimulants	10.0%	4.6%
Other opiates	9.5%	4.3%
Tranquilizers	7.3%	3.1%
Sedatives	6.5%	2.9%
Hallucinogens	6.2%	1.9%
Cocaine	5.3%	2.3%
Inhalants	4.2%	1.5%
Steroids	2.5%	1.6%
Heroin	0.9%	0.5%

Taken from: Press release: "Overall teen drug use continues gradual decline; but use of inhalants rises," University of Michigan News and Information Services, December 21, 2004.

Reflecting on the Road to Ruin

When all is said and done, those who've made it through will reflect on roads to ruin. They'll never forget the incredible rush from snorting or chewing Oxy, but memories of hitting rock bottom will resonate the loudest.

Eric remains enamored by Oxy. He raves about its euphoric properties. There's nothing tempting, however, about returning to life as an active addict.

"When you've gotten to that point where you are so morally and spiritually bankrupt, when you don't even want to live anymore, it takes more than a bad day or hearing someone talk about it or seeing a pill to make you crave it," he says. "My worst day sober is still better than my best day ever was using."

Analyze the Essay:

1. Instead of relying on facts, statistics, or historical examples the way other viewpoints in this section do to make their arguments, this viewpoint focuses on the narrative story of "Eric," a teenager who developed a devastating prescription drug addiction. In what ways does the narrative style differ? What advantages and disadvantages might there be in describing one person's personal story? Explain your answer thoroughly.

2. In your opinion, what are the most effective details in this essay? Cite examples from the text to give your answer.

Marijuana Causes Health Problems

National Institute on Drug Abuse

The following viewpoint, published by the National Institute on Drug Abuse (NIDA), argues that marijuana can damage the brain, heart, lungs, and mind of users. NIDA presents evidence that marijuana damages a user's memory, and increases a person's risk of heart attack and cancer. Studies have also shown that that marijuana lowers a user's immune system and impairs judgment and learning abilities, according to NIDA. For these reasons, NIDA concludes that marijuana should be regarded as a dangerous drug that has serious health consequences.

This viewpoint was prepared by the National Institute on Drug Abuse (NIDA), a part of the National Institute of Health, a government organization.

Consider the Following Questions:

1. According to NIDA, what effect does marijuana have on a user's risk of having a heart attack?
2. What parallels have been found between marijuana and cancer, according to the authors?
3. What did a survey of 129 college students find about marijuana's health effects, as reported by NIDA?

National Institute on Drug Abuse (NIDA), "NIDA Infofacts: Marijuana," *NIDA Infofacts*, April, 2006.

Marijuana is the most commonly abused illicit drug in the United States. A dry, shredded green/brown mix of flowers, stems, seeds, and leaves of the hemp plant Cannabis sativa, it usually is smoked as a cigarette (joint, nail), or in a pipe (bong). It also is smoked in blunts, which are cigars that have been emptied of tobacco and refilled with marijuana, often in combination with another drug. It might also be mixed in food or brewed as a tea. As a more concentrated, resinous form it is called hashish and, as a sticky black liquid, hash oil. Marijuana smoke has a pungent and distinctive, usually sweet-and-sour odor. . . .

The main active chemical in marijuana is THC (delta-9-tetrahydrocannabinol). The membranes of certain nerve cells in the brain contain protein receptors that bind to THC. Once securely in place, THC kicks off a series of cellular reactions that ultimately lead to the high that users experience when they smoke marijuana. . . .

Effects on the Brain

Scientists have learned a great deal about how THC acts in the brain to produce its many effects. When someone smokes marijuana, THC rapidly passes from the lungs into the bloodstream, which carries the chemical to organs throughout the body, including the brain.

In the brain, THC connects to specific sites called cannabinoid receptors on nerve cells and influences the activity of those cells. Some brain areas have many cannabinoid receptors; others have few or none. Many cannabinoid receptors are found in the parts of the brain that influence pleasure, memory, thought, concentration, sensory and time perception, and coordinated movement.

The short-term effects of marijuana can include problems with memory and learning; distorted perception; difficulty in thinking and problem solving; loss of coordination; and increased heart rate. Research findings for long-term marijuana abuse indicate some changes in the brain similar to those seen after long-term abuse of other major drugs. For example, cannabinoid (THC or synthetic forms of THC) withdrawal in chronically exposed animals leads to an increase in the activation of the stress-response system and changes in the activity of nerve cells containing dopamine. Dopamine neurons are involved in the regulation of motivation and reward, and are directly or indirectly affected by all drugs of abuse.

Effects on the Heart

One study has indicated that an abuser's risk of heart attack more than quadruples in the first hour after smoking marijuana. The researchers suggest that such an effect might occur from marijuana's effects on blood pressure and heart rate and reduced oxygen-carrying capacity of blood.

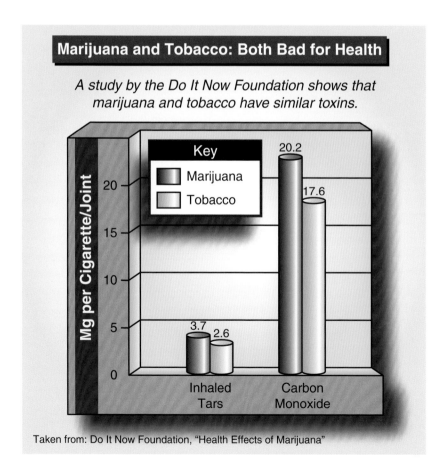

Marijuana and Tobacco: Both Bad for Health

A study by the Do It Now Foundation shows that marijuana and tobacco have similar toxins.

Taken from: Do It Now Foundation, "Health Effects of Marijuana"

Effects on the Lungs

A study of 450 individuals found that people who smoke marijuana frequently but do not smoke tobacco have more health problems and miss more days of work than non-smokers. Many of the extra sick days among the marijuana smokers in the study were for respiratory illnesses.

Even infrequent abuse can cause burning and stinging of the mouth and throat, often accompanied by a heavy cough. Someone who smokes marijuana regularly may have many of the same respiratory problems that tobacco smokers do, such as daily cough and phlegm production, more frequent acute chest illness, a heightened risk of lung infections, and a greater tendency to obstructed airways. Smoking marijuana possibly increases the likelihood of developing cancer of the head or neck. A study comparing 173 cancer patients and 176 healthy individuals produced evidence that marijuana smoking doubled or tripled the risk of these cancers.

Marijuana abuse also has the potential to promote cancer of the lungs and other parts of the respiratory tract because it contains irritants and carcinogens. In fact, marijuana smoke contains 50 to 70 percent more carcinogenic hydrocarbons than does tobacco smoke. It also induces high levels of an enzyme that converts certain hydrocarbons into their carcinogenic form—levels that may accelerate the changes that ultimately produce malignant cells. Marijuana users usually inhale more deeply and hold their breath longer than tobacco smokers do, which increases the lungs' exposure to carcinogenic smoke. These facts suggest that, puff for puff, smoking marijuana may be more harmful to the lungs than smoking tobacco.

Marijuana Causes Health Problems

The truth is, there are laws against marijuana because marijuana is harmful. With every year that passes, medical research discovers greater dangers from smoking it, from links to serious mental illness to the risk of cancer, and even dangers from in utero exposure.

John P. Walters, "No surrender: the drug war saves lives," *National Review*, September 27, 2004.

Some of marijuana's adverse health effects may occur because THC impairs the immune system's ability to fight disease. In laboratory experiments that exposed animal and human cells to THC or other marijuana ingredients, the normal disease-preventing reactions of many of the key types of immune cells were inhibited. In other studies, mice exposed to THC or related substances were more likely than unexposed mice to develop bacterial infections and tumors.

Organizations such as the National Institute on Drug Abuse (NIDA) treat substance abusers and educate them on the health risks of taking drugs.

Effects of Heavy Marijuana Use on Learning and Social Behavior

Research clearly demonstrates that marijuana has the potential to cause problems in daily life or make a person's existing problems worse. Depression, anxiety, and personality disturbances have been associated with chronic marijuana use. Because marijuana compromises the ability to

During a raid in Connecticut, a state police trooper cuts down a marijuana plant.

learn and remember information, the more a person uses marijuana the more he or she is likely to fall behind in accumulating intellectual, job, or social skills. Moreover, research has shown that marijuana's adverse impact on memory and learning can last for days or weeks after the acute effects of the drug wear off.

Students who smoke marijuana get lower grades and are less likely to graduate from high school, compared with their nonsmoking peers. A study of 129 college students found that, among those who smoked the drug at least 27 of the 30 days prior to being surveyed, critical skills related to attention, memory, and learning were significantly impaired, even after the students had not taken the drug for at least 24 hours. These "heavy" marijuana abusers had more trouble sustaining and shifting their attention and in registering, organizing, and using information than did the study participants who had abused marijuana no more than 3 of the previous 30 days. As a result, someone who smokes marijuana every day may be functioning at a reduced intellectual level all of the time.

More recently, the same researchers showed that the ability of a group of long-term heavy marijuana abusers to recall words from a list remained impaired for a week after quitting, but returned to normal within 4 weeks. Thus, some cognitive abilities may be restored in individuals who quit smoking marijuana, even after long-term heavy use.

Workers who smoke marijuana are more likely than their coworkers to have problems on the job. Several studies associate workers' marijuana smoking with increased absences, tardiness, accidents, workers' compensation claims, and job turnover. A study among postal workers found that employees who tested positive for marijuana on a pre-employment urine drug test had 55 percent more industrial accidents, 85 percent more injuries, and a 75-percent increase in absenteeism compared with those who tested negative for marijuana use. In another study, heavy marijuana abusers reported that the drug impaired several important measures of life achievement including cognitive abilities, career status, social life, and physical and mental health.

Analyze the Essay:

1. This viewpoint was prepared by an extension of the National Institute of Health, which is a government agency. Does the fact that this material was prepared by government sources influence your opinion of its credibility? Explain your reasoning.

2. The authors of this viewpoint suggest that there is a connection between marijuana and mental illness. How do you think Paul Armentano, author of the following viewpoint, would respond to that suggestion? Use evidence from the text to support your answer.

Marijuana Does Not Cause Health Problems

Paul Armentano

In this viewpoint Paul Armentano refutes claims that marijuana is a harmful drug. Armentano points to scientific studies which conclude that marijuana is relatively safe when compared to other drugs. Armentano says that although there have been some indications that marijuana may cause mental illness in specific individuals, that is no reason to regard it as dangerous. Ibuprofen, used by millions of Americans for pain relief, can cause liver and kidney problems in some Americans—but no one would suggest making ibuprofen illegal, he argues. Armentano concludes that marijuana has been demonized by the federal government's war on drugs, and is much safer than most people realize.

Paul Armentano is a senior policy analyst with the National Organization for the Reform of Marijuana Laws (NORML), a nonprofit lobbying organization that seeks to legalize marijuana.

Consider the Following Questions:

1. What evidence regarding the connection between marijuana and mental illness does the author consider to be weak?
2. Why does the author believe it is important to look at cannabis in context?
3. Why does the author believe that a connection to psychotic disorders is reason to make marijuana legally regulated?

Paul Armentano, "Cannabis, Mental Health, and Context: The Case for Regulation," *National Organization for the Reform of Marijuana Laws (NORML)*, November 1, 2006, Copyright © 2006 NORML. Reproduced by permission.

Armed with sound-bites reminiscent of the 1936 propaganda film "Reefer Madness," the US government recently kicked off yet another smear campaign on the supposed dangers of marijuana. The Feds' latest charge: Pot causes mental illness.

"A growing body of evidence now demonstrates that smoking marijuana can increase the risk of serious mental health problems," states US Drug Czar John Walters. "New research being conducted here and abroad illustrates that marijuana use, particularly during teen years, can lead to depression, thoughts of suicide, and schizophrenia."

Weak Evidence that Marijuana Causes Mental Illness

Predictably, those looking for the science behind the White House's alarm will be hard pressed to find any. Absent from government's latest campaign is any mention of a recent clinical study in the journal *Psychiatry Research* refuting a causal link between cannabis use and behavior suggestive of schizophrenia. "The current study . . . suggest[s] a temporal precedence of schizotypal traits before cannabis use in most cases," its authors conclude. "These findings do not support a causal link between cannabis use and schizotypal traits."

Comprehensive reviews by the United Kingdom's Advisory Council on the Misuse of Drugs and Britain's prestigious Beckley Foundation affirm this finding, noting that "increased rates of cannabis use in the last thirty years have not been accompanied by a corresponding increase in the rate of psychosis in the population," and warning that "at worst, . . . using cannabis [may] increase lifetime risk of developing schizophrenia by one percent."

Survey data published in the journal *Addictive Behavior* also puts a damper on the White House's "pot leads to depression" claim. After analyzing survey results from 4,400 adults who had completed The Center for Epidemiologic Studies Depression scale (a numerical, self-report scale designed to assess symptoms of depression in the general population), researchers at the University of Southern California found: "Despite comparable ranges of scores on all depression subscales, those who used once per week or less had less depressed mood, more positive affect, and fewer somatic (physical) complaints than non-users. . . . Daily users [also] reported less depressed mood and more positive affect than non-users."

"A Relatively Safe Drug"

Separate longitudinal data published in the October 2006 edition of the journal *Addiction* further rejects the claim that cannabis use is a significant predictor of depression, finding that any associations observed between self-reported

Many Americans believe that marijuana should be legalized throughout the country because of the plant's many medicinal uses.

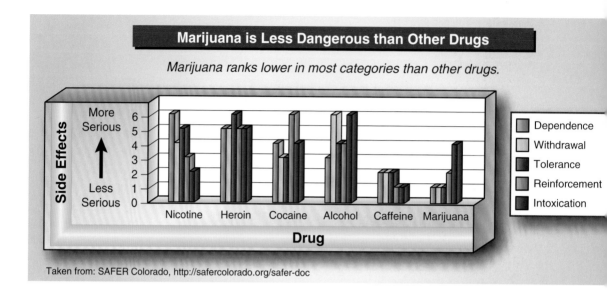

Marijuana is Less Dangerous than Other Drugs

Marijuana ranks lower in most categories than other drugs.

Legend:
- Dependence
- Withdrawal
- Tolerance
- Reinforcement
- Intoxication

Side Effects (More Serious ↑ Less Serious, scale 0–6)

Drugs: Nicotine, Heroin, Cocaine, Alcohol, Caffeine, Marijuana

Taken from: SAFER Colorado, http://safercolorado.org/safer-doc

pot use and subsequent depression are not attributable to marijuana use *per se,* but rather to "third (common) factors associated with both the decision to use marijuana and depression."

Finally, there are the conclusions of a recent meta-analysis investigating the use of cannabis use and its impact on mental health published in the journal *Current Opinion in Pharmacology.* The study's verdict? Those who use cannabis in moderation, even long- term "will not suffer any lasting physical or mental harm. . . . Overall, by comparison with other drugs used mainly for 'recreational' purposes, cannabis could be rated to be a relatively safe drug."

Cannabis in Context

The phrase "relatively safe" is appropriate in any discussion regarding cannabis and mental health. No substance is harmless and in many cases, the relative dangers of a drug may be increased or decreased depending on set and setting. Cannabis is no different.

There are a handful of longitudinal studies suggesting an association, albeit a minor one, between chronic cannabis (primarily among adolescents and/or those predisposed to mental illness) and increased symptoms of depression, psychotic symptoms, and/or schizophrenia. However, interpretation of this data is troublesome and, to date, this observed association is not well understood. Identified as well as unidentified confounding factors (such as poverty, family history, polydrug use, etc.) make it difficult, if not impossible, for researchers to unequivocally determine whether any cause-and-effect relationship exists between cannabis use and mental illness. Also, many experts point out that this association may be due to patients' self-medicating with cannabis, as survey data and anecdotal reports of individuals finding therapeutic relief from both clinical depression and schizotypal behavior are common within medical lore, and clinical testing on the use of cannabinoids to treat certain symptoms of mental illness has been recommended.

Nevertheless, until this association is better understood, there may be some merit in the government's caution that adolescents (particularly pre and early teens) and/or adults with pre-existing symptoms of mental illness refrain from using marijuana (and/or other psychoactive substances), particularly in large quantities. This statement, however, is hardly an indictment of marijuana's relative safety when used in moderation by adults or an endorsement of the federal government's efforts to criminally prohibit its use for all Americans. If anything, just the opposite is true.

Marijuana Should Not Be Prohibited

Health risks connected with drug use—when scientifically documented—should not be seen as legitimate reasons for criminal prohibition, but instead, as reasons for legal regulation. Specific to cannabis, if as the Drug Czar alleges, studies demonstrate that those "who first used marijuana before age 12 [are] twice as likely as adults who first used marijuana at age 18 or older to be classified as having serious mental illness," then this is an argument in favor of legally regulating cannabis in a manner similar to alcohol, so that better safeguards may be enacted restricting adolescents from legal access to it. Walters' concerns, however, do not support criminally prohibiting the responsible use of the cannabis by adults any more than fears regarding the abuse of alcohol by a minority of teenagers support a blanket prohibition on the use of beer by adults.

In addition, if as the Drug Czar questionably suggests, "as many as one in four people may have a genetic profile that makes marijuana five times more likely to trigger psychotic disorders," this claim is yet another argument in favor of regulation. If there does exist a minority population of citizens who may be genetically prone to potential harms from cannabis (such as, possibly, those predisposed to schizophrenia), then a regulated system would best identify and educate this subpopulation to pot's potential risks so that they may refrain from its use, if they so choose.

Marijuana as Medicine

One of THC's [the active ingedient in marijuana] medical uses best supported by research is the treatment of nausea. It can improve mild to moderate nausea caused by cancer chemotherapy and help reduce nausea and weight loss in people with AIDS.

"Marijuana as medicine: Consider the pros and cons," The Mayo Clinic.com, August 25, 2006.

Just Because Some Are at Risk Does Not Mean a Substance Is Dangerous

To draw a real world comparison, millions of Americans safely use ibuprofen as an effective pain reliever. However, among a minority of the population who suffer from liver and kidney problems, ibuprofen presents a legitimate and substantial health risk. However, this fact no more calls for the criminalization of ibuprofen among adults than do the Drug Czar's half-baked claims, even if true, call for the current prohibition of cannabis.

Finally, there lies the fact that cannabis prohibition has forever undermined the federal government's ability to educate its citizens, particularly young people, to the potential risks of marijuana when and where they present themselves. Ending prohibition and enacting a legal, regulated cannabis

market would likely restore this lost credibility, as evidenced by the fact that science-based, federal education campaigns regarding the health risks of tobacco and drunk driving have greatly reduced smoking and driving under the influence among teenagers. Conversely, similar rhetorically-based campaigns regarding teen pot use have fostered increased levels of illicit drug use among their target audience.

As concluded by the Netherlands Drug Policy Foundation, cannabis' "health risks are remarkably limited, but cannabis is not completely harmless." As a result, the Foundation determined: "There ought to he a special legal regulatory system for cannabis because its use definitely does entail health risks. If cannabis was completely harmless, the same rules could be applied as to tea. Cannabis should not be made freely available, but the rules on cannabis can be very

Marijuana can bring relief for people suffering from diseases. Bill Britt, executive director of the Association of Patient Advocates, uses marijuana to ease pain from epilepsy and post-polio syndrome.

general and lenient." Placed in this context, the administration's latest anti-pot campaign does little to advance the government's position in favor of tightening prohibition, and provides ample ammunition to wage for its repeal.

Analyze the Essay:

1. The author of this viewpoint and the author of the opposing viewpoint both contend that science is on their side. They each point to scientific studies to back their claims. In your opinion, which author is more convincing about whether marijuana is harmful to health?

2. Paul Armentano refers to marijuana as a "relatively safe drug." How do you think the authors of the previous viewpoint would respond to that description?

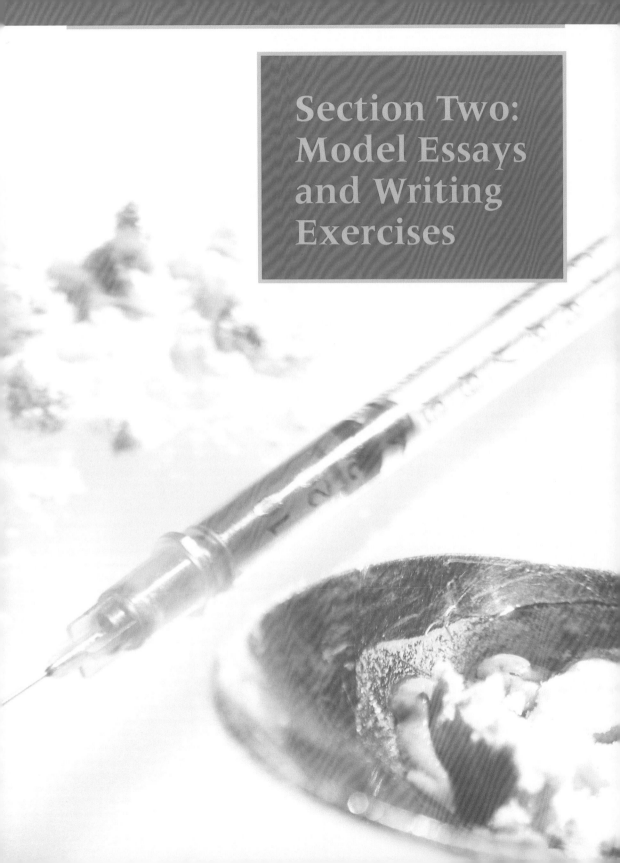

Section Two:
Model Essays
and Writing
Exercises

The Five-Paragraph Essay

An *essay* is a short piece of writing that discusses or analyzes one topic. The five-paragraph essay is a form commonly used in school assignments and tests. Every five-paragraph essay begins with an *introduction,* ends with a *conclusion,* and features three *supporting paragraphs* in the middle.

The Thesis Statement. The introduction includes the essay's thesis statement. The thesis statement presents the argument or point the author is trying to make about the topic. The essays in this book all have different thesis statements because they are making different arguments about drug abuse.

The thesis statement should clearly tell the reader what the essay will be about. A focused thesis statement helps determine what will be in the essay; the subsequent paragraphs are spent developing and supporting its argument.

The Introduction. In addition to presenting the thesis statement, a well-written introductory paragraph captures the attention of the reader and explains why the topic being explored is important. It may provide the reader with background information on the subject matter or feature an anecdote that illustrates a point relevant to the topic. It could also present startling information that clarifies the point of the essay or put forth a contradictory position that the essay will refute. Further techniques for writing an introduction are found later in this section.

The Supporting Paragraphs. The introduction is then followed by three (or more) supporting paragraphs. These are the main body of the essay. Each paragraph presents and develops a subtopic that supports the essay's thesis statement. Each subtopic is spearheaded by a topic sentence and supported by details, and examples. The writer can use various kinds of supporting material and details to back up the topic of each supporting paragraph. These may include statistics, quotations from people with special knowledge or expertise, historic facts, and anecdotes. A rule of writing is that specific and concrete examples are more convincing than vague, general, or unsupported assertions.

The Conclusion. The *conclusion* is the paragraph that closes the essay. Its function is to summarize or reiterate the main idea of the essay. It may recall an idea from the introduction or briefly examine the larger implications of the thesis. Because the conclusion is also the last chance a writer has to make an impression on the reader, it is important that it not simply repeat what has been presented elsewhere in the essay but close it in a clear, final, and memorable way.

Although the order of the essay's component paragraphs is important, they do not have to be written in the order presented here. Some writers like to decide on a thesis and write the introduction paragraph first. Other writers like to focus first on the body of the essay, and write the introduction and conclusion later.

Pitfalls to Avoid

When writing essays about controversial issues such as drug abuse, it is important to remember that disputes over the material are common precisely because there are many different perspectives. Remember to state your arguments in careful and measured terms. Evaluate your topic fairly—avoid overstating negative qualities of one perspective or understating positive qualities of another. Use examples, facts, and details to support any assertions you make.

The Cause-and-Effect Essay

The previous section of this book provided you with samples of published persuasive writing on drug abuse. All were persuasive, or opinion, essays making certain arguments about drug abuse. They were also either cause-and-effect essays or used cause-and-effect reasoning. This section will focus on writing your own cause-and-effect essays.

Cause and effect is a common method of organizing and explaining ideas and events. Simply put, cause and effect is a relationship between two things in which one thing makes something else happen. The *cause* is the reason why something happens. The *effect* is what happens as a result.

A simple example would be a car not starting because it is out of gas. The lack of gas is the cause; the failure to start is the effect. Another example of cause-and-effect reasoning is found in the quote box accompanying Viewpoint Three. Author Diana Mahoney describes how peer pressure—the pressure on students to succeed academically, athletically, and socially—is causing students to use enhancement-performing drugs such as steroids in order to "get strong, to get lean, to get validation, and to get scholarships."[1] The pressure is the cause; teen steroid use is the effect.

Not all cause-and-effect relationships are as clear-cut as these two examples. It can be difficult to determine the cause of an effect, especially when talking about broad societal issues. For example, smoking and tobacco have been long associated with each other, but not all cancer patients smoke, and not all smokers get cancer. It took decades of debate and research before the U.S. Surgeon General concluded in 1964 that smoking cigarettes caused cancer (and even then, that conclusion was disputed by tobacco com-

[1] Diane Mahoney, "Teens and Steroids: A Dangerous Mix," *Clinical Psychiatry News*, June 2006, p. 50.

panies for many years thereafter). Similarly, in Viewpoint One, author Jonathan Last argues that the "Just Say No" program helped reduce the problem of teen drug abuse. In 1979, Last says that 31.8 percent of 12- to 17-year-olds had used drugs; as a result of "Just Say No," by 1993 only 16.4 percent of teens that age had used drugs. His argument is that the "Just Say No" program was the cause; reducing teen drug use was the effect. Whether the drug use decline is in fact directly attributable to the "Just Say No" program is debatable, however—other factors, such as lack of drug supply, could also explain the drop in teen drug use. Creating and evaluating cause and effect involves both collecting and proving evidence and exercising critical thinking.

Types of Cause-and-Effect Essays

In general, there are three types of cause-and-effect essays. In one type, many causes can contribute to a single effect. Supporting paragraphs would each examine one specific cause. For example, Jonathan Last in Viewpoint One argues that several efforts, including the "Just Say No" program, an increase of federal funding, and fruitful drug raids, have resulted in the success of the War on Drugs. The programs, funding, and drug raids are the causes; together they have resulted in a successful War on Drugs—the effect.

Another type of cause-and-effect essay examines multiple effects from a single cause. The thesis posits that one event or circumstance has multiple results. An example from this volume is found in Viewpoint Four by the National Institute on Drug Abuse (NIDA). NIDA argues that a single cause, marijuana use, can have multiple health effects on users, including damaging the brain and lungs, increasing a person's risk of heart attack and cancer, impairing judgment, learning abilities, and memories. Marijuana use is the single cause; a variety of health problems are the multiple effects.

A final type of cause-and-effect essay is one that examines a series of causes and effects—a "chain of events" in which each link is both the effect of what happened before and the cause of what happens next. Jamie Gadette in Viewpoint Three provides one example. She describes the story of Eric, who begins using drugs recreationally at parties. This initial experience with drugs (a cause) triggered Eric to fall deeper into the world of drugs (an effect). Using small amounts of the drug OxyContin led to him needing larger amounts; needing larger amounts led him to need money from sources other than his job. He began stealing petty items and borrowing money from his family; his family's involvement in his drug habit led them to hold an intervention, in which Eric was forced to go to rehab. This is one example of a chain of events sequence in which an initial cause can have successive repercussions down the line.

Tips to Remember

In writing argumentative essays about controversial issues such as drug abuse, it is important to remember disputes over cause-and-effect relationships are part of the controversy. Drug abuse is a complex phenomenon that has multiple effects and multiple causes, and often there is disagreement over what causes what. One needs to be careful and measured in how arguments are expressed. Avoid overstating cause-and-effect relationships if they are unwarranted.

Another pitfall to avoid in writing cause-and-effect essays is to mistake chronology for causation. The fact that event X came before event Y does not necessarily mean that X *caused* Y. Additional evidence may be needed, such as documented studies or similar testimony from many people. Likewise, correlation does not necessarily imply causation. Just because two events happened at the same time does not necessarily mean they are causally related. Again, additional evidence is needed to verify the cause/effect argument.

In the following section, you will read some model essays on drug abuse that use cause-and-effect arguments and complete exercises that will help you write your own.

Words and Phrases Common in Cause-and-Effect Essays

accordingly

as a result of

because

consequently

due to

for

for this reason

it then follows that

if…then

so

so that

since

subsequently

therefore

this is how

thus

Discovering the Causes of Teenage Drug Abuse

Editor's Notes The first model essay examines the multiple causes of teen drug abuse. The author argues that peer pressure, athletic pressure, and a variety of depressive disorders contribute to a tendency in teens to use and abuse drugs. The essay is structured as a five-paragraph essay in which each paragraph contributes a supporting piece of evidence to develop the argument.

The notes in the margin point out key features of the essay, and will help you understand how the essay is organized. Also note that all sources are cited using Modern Language Association (MLA) style. For more information on how to cite your sources see Appendix C*. In addition, consider the following:

1. How does the introduction engage the reader's attention?
2. What cause-and-effect techniques are used in the essay?
3. What purpose do the essay's quotes serve?
4. Does the essay convince you of its point?

Refers to thesis and topic sentences

Refers to supporting details

Paragraph 1

The introductory paragraph establishes the problem of teen drug abuse before addressing the problem's cause.

Drug abuse is an enduring problem among American teenagers. According to teen drug abuse expert Meredith Moran, nearly 66 percent of American teenagers do drugs before they finish high school, and 25 percent of high school seniors have problems with drugs and alcohol. According to author Dave Marcus, the author of *What It Takes to Pull Me Through: Why Teenagers Get in Trouble and How Four of*

*In applying MLA style guidelines in this book, the following simplifications have been made: Parenthetical text citations are confined to direct quotations only; electronic source documentation in the Works Cited list omits date of access, page ranges, and some detailed facts of publication.

Them Got Out, testified that in 2007 there existed a record number of schools especially reserved for kids dealing with problems of substance abuse—as many as 100,000 students in more than 300 schools across the country. Understanding why teenagers abuse drugs is the first step to addressing this problem. When considering the problem of teen drug abuse, it is important to recognize that there is no single cause; several causes may act in concert to push a young person towards drugs.

This is the essay's thesis statement.

Paragraph 2

A main cause of teenage drug abuse is peer pressure. Teens are exceedingly vulnerable to succumbing to peer pressure, which is when a person engages in an activity—even a dangerous one—out of a desire to fit in. As author Helen Cordes explains, "Just about any girl finds it hard to resist going along with peer norms, so when her friends are doing dangerous things, it's hard for a girl who may be under stress already to go against the tide." As teens earn their freedom with later curfews and drivers' licenses, they are more likely to attend parties at which peer pressure can be at its peak. Said one teenager of her experience, "I didn't want to look stupid . . . so I started smoking pot. . . . One night at a party I tried E[cstasy]. . . . Now, I'm 16 years old and I just got out of rehab for cocaine and ecstasy. Take it from me. It really isn't worth it." (qtd. In "Kid's Eye View")

This is the topic sentence of paragraph 2. Topic sentences can be simple and clear.

Paragraph 3

Young people increasingly face another form of pressure; a daunting expectation to look strong, healthy, and beautiful, and be physically able to perform their best. However, becoming a top-performing high school athlete or bronzed, buff, beauty queen does not come naturally to everyone. For this reason, an increasing number of students—both male and female—are turning to performance-enhancing

This transitional phrase allows the author to fluidly move from one idea to the next.

drugs such as steroids in order to excel in athletic competi-
tions and increase their physical image. Indeed, the National
Institute on Drug Abuse estimates more than half a million
8th- and 10th-graders use steroids annually. Performing
and appearing a certain way is exceedingly important in
America's increasingly appearance-driven student bodies.
Author Diana Mahoney, who has studied the issue of teenage steroid abuse in depth, warns educators, coaches, and
parents to watch for drug abuse in "the high-performing
student athletes who do their families proud, the perfectionist fitness buffs whose internal personas become defined
by their external appearance, and the little guys who know
that the big guys get all the attention and all of the dates."
Indeed, the pressure to have big muscles and flat abdomi-
nals is driving a growing number of teens to view steroids
as harmless, when in reality they have serious and lasting
health affects.

Paragraph 4

Finally, a third condition that makes teenagers likely to
become addicted to drugs is depression. Kids who feel left
out socially, who come from depressing or challenging family
lives, or who struggle with eating disorders such as anorexia
and bulimia, are all more likely to try and become addicted to
drugs. According to the National Institute of Mental Health,
"A lot of depressed people, especially teenagers, have problems with alcohol or other drugs. . . . Sometimes the depression comes first and people try drugs as a way to escape it.
(In the long run, drugs or alcohol just make things worse!)
Other times, the alcohol or other drug use comes first, and
depression is caused by: the drug itself, or withdrawal from
it, or the problems that substance use causes." Although
teenagers may think that drugs or alcohol make them feel
happy or help them forget about their problems, over time
drug abuse only worsens their depression.

Paragraph 5

While not the only causes of teen drug abuse, the pressure to fit in, the pressure to be physically superior, and depression play a strong role in pushing teenagers to use and abuse drugs. Understanding why teenagers turn to drugs is a first step towards getting them the help they need. "We can still do things like set limits and enforce rules," says Marcus, "but we have to really listen first." (qtd. in Cordes)

The author established Marcus as an authority on this subject at the beginning of the essay.

Works Cited

"Kid's Eye View," *Parents. The Anti-Drug* 27 Feb 2007 www.theantidrug.com/community/ktopics.asp?topic = 4

"Let's Talk About Depression," National Institute of Mental Health 17 Feb 2006 http://www.nimh.nih.gov/publicat/letstalk.cfm.

Cordes, Helen. "When You're Afraid of Losing Her." *Daughter,* Jan/Feb 2006. Vol 11, Iss. 1.

Mahoney, Diana. "Teens and Steroids: A Dangerous Mix." *Clinical Psychiatry News* June 2006: 50.

Exercise 1A: Create an Outline from an Existing Essay

It often helps to create an outline of the five-paragraph essay before you write it. The outline can help you organize the information, arguments, and evidence you have gathered during your research.

For this exercise, create an outline that could have been used to write "Discovering the Causes of Teenage Drug Abuse." This "reverse engineering" exercise is meant to help familiarize you with how outlines can help classify and arrange information.

To do this you will need to
1. articulate the essay's thesis;
2. pinpoint important pieces of evidence;
3. flag quotes that supported the essay's ideas; and
4. identify key points that supported the argument.

Part of the outline has already been started to give you an idea of the assignment.

Outline

I. Paragraph One

A. Write the essay's thesis:

II. Paragraph Two

Topic: Peer pressure contributes to teen drug abuse.

A.

B. Parties are a place where teens feel peer pressure to try drugs. Quote provides an example of one teenage drug addiction that began at a party.

III. Paragraph Three

Topic: Pressure to look strong, healthy, and beautiful, and be physically able to perform their best causes some teenagers to use drugs.

A. National Institute on Drug Abuse statistic quantifies teenage steroid abuse

B.

IV. Paragraph Four

Topic:

A.

B.

V. Paragraph Five

A. Write the essay's conclusion:

The Consequences of Drug Abuse

Editor's Notes The second model essay embodies a different form of cause-and-effect essay: multiple effects from a single cause. The thesis posits that one event or circumstance has multiple results. In the case of this essay, the author argues that drug abuse can have multiple effects on a person's life. In clear, distinct paragraphs the author outlines an effect that drug abuse has on a user's life, and supports her points with facts, anecdotes, and quotes.

As you read this essay, take note of its components and how they are organized (the sidebars in the margins provide further explanation).

Refers to thesis and topic sentences

Refers to supporting details

What is the essay's thesis statement?

Paragraph 1

It is common for drug addicts to lose everything good in their lives because of their addiction. But unfortunately, few drug addicts consider how their drug habit will affect their personal lives before becoming addicted. Indeed, using drugs can have multiple effects on a user's life. Drug abuse can be devastating, draining a person of their personality, robbing them of their health, making them unrecognizable to family and friends, consuming their assets, and damaging their community.

Paragraph 2

Drug users pay a heavy price for their habit: their health. According to the Office of National Drug Control Policy, prolonged use of cocaine causes respiratory problems such as coughing, shortness of breath, severe chest pains, and can cause bleeding in the lungs and nasal passages. Heroin use causes collapsed veins, infection of the heart lining and valves, abscesses, and liver disease, and also exposes users to communicable diseases such as hepatitis and AIDS. Methamphetamine use causes convulsions, paranoia, extreme weight loss, memory loss, visual and auditory hallucinations, delusions, and severe dental problems. An overdose of any of these drugs can cause death. Even marijuana, widely regarded as less harmful than harder drugs, can cause "acute chest illness, a heightened risk of lung infection, and a heightened risk of . . . developing cancer of the head or neck." (National Institute on Drug Abuse, 3)

What authorities are cited? What do they offer the essay?

Paragraph 3

As users become increasingly consumed by an addiction, they tend to pull away from the people who love them most: their friends and family. Because their top priority becomes obtaining drugs and getting high, they withdraw from social activities, hobbies, and responsibilities, and often become completely unrecognizable to their loved ones. One mother described the transformation her drug-addicted son Anthony underwent: "His handsome smile had disappeared into a scowl. His speech was slurred, and he was sullen and glum. At times he'd become so angry he would throw things, fighting the demons he thought were winning." (Gatlin) Witnessing their son, daughter, brother or husband fall to such depths is endlessly painful for family members and friends who feel like there is little they can do to help their loved one.

Using first-hand narratives, such as this quote, can lend a personal voice to your essay.

Paragraph 4

Another dark affect of drug abuse is the toll it takes on a user's finances. Many users resort to petty theft, even from loved ones, to sustain their drug habit. They may lose jobs, sell valuables, or prostitute themselves just to fuel their drug supply. In addition to the user's finances, drug abuse takes a toll on a community's resources and finances. Indeed, drug addicts tend to bring crime and violence into neighborhoods as they steal and rob to feed their habit. And, while attending a rehabilitation program is a positive step, such programs

What transitional phrases are employed in this essay? On a separate sheet of paper, list them all.

What facts are used to support the essay? Are they effective, in your opinion?

are expensive and are often paid for by community organizations or employers of drug addicts. Furthermore, drug addicts drain resources when they need medical treatment: the Drug Abuse Warning Network (DAWN) estimated that in 2004 there were more than 1.2 million emergency room visits in the U.S. due to drug overdose—prescription drug abuse caused 495,732 visits, cocaine caused 383,350 visits, marijuana caused 215,665 visits and heroin caused 162,137 visits. Such visits not only cost taxpayers money but overcrowd hospitals, preventing other sick people from receiving treatment. As one drug abuse expert puts it, "Whether you indulge or not, you're paying for the party." In fact, notes the author, "drug abuse costs the U.S. economy $414 billion a year." (Maran, 9)

Paragraph 5

Rather than merely repeating the points made in the essay, the conclusion brings the ideas to a close.

These are just some of the consequences from prolonged drug abuse. Although many users think their drug problem is their personal business, clearly it affects their family, friends, and even those in their community who do not know them. Those considering trying drugs must realize how much they—and their communities—have to lose.

Works Cited

Gatlin, June Juliet. "Loving my Son to Life." *Essence* May 1994.

Maran, Meredith. *Dirty: A Search for Answers Inside America's Teenage Drug Epidemic.* San Francisco: HarperSanFrancisco, 2003: 9.

"NIDA Infofacts: Marijuana." *National Institute on Drug Abuse* April 2006: 1–8.

Exercise 2A: Create an Outline from an Existing Essay

As you did for the first model essay in this section, create an outline that could have been used to write *The Consequences of Drug Abuse*. Be sure to identify the essay's thesis statement, its supporting ideas, its descriptive passages, and key pieces of evidence that were used.

Exercise 2B: Create an Outline for Your Own Essay

The second model essay expresses a particular point of view about drug abuse. For this exercise, your assignment is to find supporting ideas, choose specific and concrete details, create an outline, and ultimately write a five-paragraph essay making a different, or even opposing, point about drug abuse. Your goal is to use cause-and-effect techniques to convince your reader.

Step I: Write a thesis statement.
The following thesis statement would be appropriate for a multiple effects essay on benefits of marijuana use:

> *Instead of being a dangerous drug that can ruin a person's life, marijuana can have many health benefits for the right user.*

Or see the sample paper topics suggested in Appendix D for more ideas.

Step II: Brainstorm pieces of supporting evidence.

Using information from some of the viewpoints in the previous section and from the information found in Section III of this book, write down three arguments or pieces of evidence that support the thesis statement you selected. Then, for each of these three arguments, write down supportive facts, examples, and details that support it. These could be:

- statistical information
- personal memories and anecdotes
- quotes from experts, peers, or family members
- observations of people's actions and behaviors
- specific and concrete details

Supporting pieces of evidence for the above sample thesis statement are found in this book, and include:

- The Mayo Clinic quote embedded in Viewpoint 5 that testifies to marijuana's use as a medicine: "One of THC's [the active ingredient in marijuana] medical uses best supported by research is the treatment of nausea. It can improve mild to moderate nausea caused by cancer chemotherapy and help reduce nausea and weight loss in people with AIDS."
- Appendix A contains information showing that several state governments have recognized the health benefits of marijuana. As of June 2006, eleven states have medical marijuana laws that make it permissible for people with certain debilitating diseases to grow or possess marijuana.

Step III: Place the information from Step II in outline form.

Step IV: Write the arguments or supporting statements in paragraph form.

By now you have three arguments that support the paragraph's thesis statement, as well as supporting material. Use the outline to write out your three supporting arguments in paragraph form. Make sure each paragraph has a topic sentence that states the paragraph's thesis clearly and broadly. Then add supporting sentences that express the facts, quotes, details, and examples that support the paragraph's argument. The paragraph may also have a concluding or summary sentence.

Marijuana Is a Gateway Drug

Editor's Notes The following essay illustrates the third type of cause-and-effect essay: a "chain of events" or "domino effect" essay in which each link is both the effect of what happened before and the cause of what happens next. It examines multiple causes of a single event or phenomenon, but the causes are sequential. In other words, instead of factors A, B, and C causing phenomenon X, this "chain of events" essay describes how A causes B, which then causes C, which in turn creates X. Chronology—expressing what events come before and which after—plays an important part in this type of essay.

This essay also differs from the previous model essays in that it is longer than five paragraphs. Sometimes five paragraphs are simply not enough to adequately develop an idea. Extending the length of an essay can allow the reader to explore a topic in more depth or present multiple pieces of evidence that together provide a complete picture of a topic. Longer essays can also help readers discover the complexity of a subject by examining a topic beyond its superficial exterior. Moreover, the ability to write a sustained research or position paper is a valuable skill you will need as you advance academically.

As you read, consider the questions posed in the margins. Continue to identify thesis statements, supporting details, transitions, and quotations. Examine the introductory and concluding paragraphs to understand how they give shape to the essay. Finally, evaluate the essay's general structure and assess its overall effectiveness.

Refers to thesis and topic sentences

Refers to supporting details

Paragraph 1

How dangerous is marijuana? While some see marijuana as a mild, non-addictive substance that can be casually used for years, in reality marijuana as an unhealthy, dangerous drug that makes users more likely to try and become addicted to even more dangerous substances such as cocaine, heroin, methamphetamines, and ecstasy. Indeed, evidence that marijuana is a "gateway" drug is found in numerous studies; a recent study of 300 sets of twins reported in the *Journal of the American Medical Association,* for example, revealed that marijuana-using twins were four times more likely than their non-using siblings to use cocaine and five times more likely to use LSD. But even more powerful evidence that marijuana is a gateway drug is found in the stories of regular people who have fallen down the slippery slope of drug use. Consider the case of one young person named Carl Smith.[1] Over time, Carl's experimentation with marijuana led to a series of terrible events that irrevocably changed his life.

> What is the essay's thesis statement?

> What phrases in paragraph 1 indicate that what follows will be a cause-and-effect essay?

Paragraph 2

Carl grew up in sunny Southern California and attended a high school in San Diego. He was a good student, performing well in school and participating in after school activities such as baseball and surfing. At the beginning of Carl's junior year in high school, however, he began attending parties where marijuana was present. Although he was wary of trying the drug, Carl did it anyway under peer pressure from his friends. "I didn't think it was a big deal," he said, "and everyone else was doing it. I didn't want to look like a loser." (qtd. in Friedman) Carl is not alone in his experience; the National Institute on Drug Abuse reports that nearly 45 percent of U.S. teenagers try marijuana before finishing high school.

> What idea does this fact support?

---

[1] His name has been changed to protect his identity.

Paragraph 3

Carl was intrigued by his first experience with marijuana; contrary to what he'd been taught in drug education classes, he didn't feel depressed or psychotic. He had simply enjoyed the experience of getting high. Indeed, attempting to scare young people away from drugs by exaggerating their consequences—a common anti-drug strategy—can often result in their increased use. In fact, students in one anti-drug study "discounted or outright rejected [exaggerated] ads because they knew people who were using (or maybe were using themselves) and weren't seeing the consequences depicted. . . . [Such students begin to see all anti-drug education as] one big con job." (Asper, 18) Figuring that other information he had been given about drugs was similarly untrue, Carl began using marijuana regularly at parties. By the beginning of his senior year, he was getting high after school on weekdays; mid-semester he was smoking pot at lunch. Carl quickly became one of the 20 percent of high school seniors that the University of Michigan found uses marijuana on a regular monthly basis.

This fact was taken from Appendix A. Learn how to use credible statistics to support your points and claims.

Paragraph 4

As Carl's pot habit became more regular, he found he needed more and more of the drug to get the same high he had once experienced. A friend suggested that he try something stronger, such as LSD, ecstasy, or cocaine. At first Carl declined—after all, he had never pictured himself using hard drugs. "But how much different from marijuana could they be?" he reasoned. "I figured it wouldn't be a big deal to try it." (qtd. in Friedman) And with that step, Carl's marijuana habit had ushered him into the world of hard drugs. Again, Carl's experience was not unique; according to the National Center on Substance Abuse and Addiction at Columbia University, teenagers who have used marijuana in the past 30 days are 13 times more likely to use another drug, such as cocaine, heroin, methamphetamines, LSD, or Ecstasy, than teens who have not used marijuana in the

What cause-and-effect chain of events is described in paragraph 4?

same time period. Furthermore, such teens are 26 times *more likely* to use a hard drug than teens who have never smoked marijuana. "The message is clear: marijuana use is not only dangerous in and of itself, it is an alarm that signals a higher risk of other drug use." ("Non-Medical Marijuana II," 16)

Paragraph 5

Marijuana's gateway effect is so serious that it caused Scott Burns, Deputy Director for State and Local Affairs in the White House Office of National Drug Control Policy (ONDCP) in 2003, to call for greater attention to the issue. "The truth is that marijuana is a gateway drug for many people," wrote Burns in a letter to professionals around the United States. "Not every person that uses marijuana will go on to use other drugs, but the overwhelming majority of people using other dangerous drugs—about 99%—began by smoking 'a little weed.'" (qtd. in "Marijuana Offenses to be Prioritized, NDAA") According to Burns, people who used marijuana are eight times more likely to have used cocaine, fifteen times more likely to have used heroin, and five times more likely to develop a need for treatment of abuse or dependence on any drug. Indeed, this is exactly what happened to Carl—after sampling cocaine and ecstasy, he became addicted to methamphetamines and pain killers such as OxyContin.

> What voices are quoted in this essay? What makes them qualified to speak on this topic? Make a list of all people quoted and their credentials.

Paragraph 6

As a result of his drug habit, Carl frequently skipped class and failed to turn in homework assignments or show up for tests. His grades fell drastically, and just three months shy of his high school graduation he was put on academic probation. Failing grades are typical of drug-using students: the National Survey on Drug Use and Health reports that students with an average grade of "D" or below were four times as likely to have used marijuana in the past year as students who reported an average grade of "A." Discouraged, Carl stopped attending school altogether. In addition to not being

> What is the topic sentence of paragraph 6?

interested in his classes, he spent most of his time with other drug users, most of whom were not in school.

Paragraph 7

Without school to fill his day, Carl began doing even more drugs, and soon needed a way to pay for them. He tried borrowing money from family members, but they refused, thinking that if he could not get money he could not continue his drug habit. So Carl started stealing from his very own family: twenty-dollar bills from his mother's wallet, even his younger sister's babysitting savings. Resorting to theft, even from family members, is common for drug addicts who have lost perspective and connection to their loved ones. The same thing happened to a Utah youth named Eric, who at first began borrowing money from his father and grandmother, and then stealing, until his family cut him off. To get money, Eric "pawned prized possessions, committed petty theft and even sold Oxy[contin] for a while." (Gadette, 22)

Specific, vivid details help drive your point home to the reader.

List all of the transitional phrases and words used in the essay thus far.

Paragraph 8

After his parents caught him stealing, they threw Carl out of the house. He found himself alone, living on the streets, not caring about anything but getting high. After 6 weeks, Carl hit rock bottom and was arrested for breaking into an electronics store. Looking back, however, Carl realizes this is the best thing that could have happened to him. "I needed something like that to happen," he admitted. "I needed something to just like, hit me, wake me up, take me out of that terrible life." (qtd. in Friedman) After serving time in a juvenile facility and undergoing an extensive rehabilitation program, Carl moved back in with his family. At the age of 20 he received his high school diploma and is attending community college with the hopes of being a computer programmer. "I got lucky," he says of his experiences. "I could have died, or screwed up my life beyond repair. I never thought I could slip so far down the cliff—but if it could happen to me, it could happen to anyone." (qtd. in Friedman)

Paragraph 9

Carl's story bears witness to marijuana's ability to become a gateway drug for certain users. While not everyone who tries marijuana will end up like Carl, or Eric, their stories testify to the devastating power of drugs, even in small doses. As Howard Simon, of the Partnership for a Drug-Free America, puts it, "The one thing everyone should be able to agree on is that for young kids, to be even 'dabbling' with marijuana is just not a good idea." (qtd. in Narconon)

After reading the essay, do you agree with the author that marijuana is a gateway drug? Why or why not?

Works Cited

Asper, Kathy. "Scared Straight? Why to Avoid Scare Tactics." *Prevention Forum Magzine* Summer 2006: 18.

Friedman, Lauri S. Interview of Carl Smith 12 Mar. 2007.

Gadette, Jamie. "The Real OC." *Salt Lake City Weekly* Vol. 22, no. 1 26 May 2005: 22.

"Marijuana Is Gateway Drug." Narconon 2001. http://www.marijuanaaddiction.info/news-left.htm?aid = 49 Accessed March 12, 2007.

"Marijuana Offenses to be Prioritized, NDAA." Northwest Center for Health & Safety 6 Feb. 2003. http://drugand-healthinfo.org/page06.php?ID = 124 Accessed March 6, 2007.

National Center on Substance Abuse and Addiction at Columbia University. "Non-Medical Marijuana II: Rite of Passage or Russian Roulette?" Apr. 2004: 16. www.casacolumbia.org/supportcasa/item/asp?cID = 12&PID = 83. Accessed February 24, 2007.

Exercise 3A: Examining Introductions and Conclusions

Every essay features introductory and concluding paragraphs that are used to frame the main ideas being presented. Along with presenting the essay's thesis statement, well-written introductions should grab the attention of the reader and make clear why the topic being explored is important. The conclusion reiterates the essay's thesis and is also the last chance for the writer to make an impression on the reader. Strong introductions and conclusions can greatly enhance an essay's effect on an audience.

The Introduction

There are several techniques that can be used to craft an introductory paragraph. An essay can start with:

- an anecdote: a brief story that illustrates a point relevant to the topic;
- startling information: facts or statistics that elucidate the point of the essay;
- setting up and knocking down a position: a position or claim believed by proponents of one side of a controversy, followed by statements that challenge that claim;
- historical perspective: an example of the way things used to be that leads into a discussion of how or why things work differently now;
- summary information: general introductory information about the topic that feeds into the essay's thesis statement.

Problem One

Reread the introductory paragraphs of the model essays and of the viewpoints in Section I. Identify which of the techniques described above are used in the example essays. How do they grab the attention of the reader? Are their thesis statements clearly presented?

Problem Two

Write an introduction for the essay you have outlined and partially written in Exercise 2B using one of the techniques described above.

The Conclusion

The conclusion brings the essay to a close by summarizing or returning to its main ideas. Good conclusions, however, go beyond simply repeating these ideas. Strong conclusions explore a topic's broader implications and reiterate why it is important to consider. They may frame the essay by returning to an anecdote featured in the opening paragraph. Alternatively, they may close with a quotation or refer back to an event in the essay. In opinionated essays, the conclusion can reiterate which side the essay is taking or ask the reader to reconsider a previously held position on the subject.

Problem Three

Reread the concluding paragraphs of the model essays and of the viewpoints in Section I. Which were most effective in driving their arguments home to the reader? What sorts of techniques did they use to do this? Did they appeal emotionally to the reader, or bookend an idea or event referenced elsewhere in the essay?

Problem Four

Write a conclusion for the essay you have outlined and partially written in Exercise 2B using one of the techniques described above.

Exercise 3B: Using Quotations to Enliven Your Essay

No essay is complete without quotations. Get in the habit of using quotes to support at least some of the ideas in your essays. Quotes do not need to appear in every paragraph, but often enough so that the essay contains voices aside from your own. When you write, use quotations to accomplish the following:

- Provide expert advice that you are not necessarily in the position to know about.
- Cite lively or passionate passages.
- Include a particularly well-written point that gets to the heart of the matter.
- Supply statistics or facts that have been derived from someone's research.
- Deliver anecdotes that illustrate the point you are trying to make.
- Express first-person testimony.

Problem One
Reread the essays presented in all sections of this book and find at least one example of each of the above quotation types.

There are a couple of important things to remember when using quotations.

- Note your sources' qualifications and biases. This way your reader can identify the person you have quoted and can put their words in a context.
- Put any quoted material within proper quotation marks. Failing to attribute quotes to their authors constitutes plagiarism, which is when an author takes someone else's words or ideas and presents them as their own. Plagiarism is a very serious infraction and must be avoided at all costs.

Write Your Own Cause-and-Effect Five-Paragraph Essay

Using the information from this book, write your own five-paragraph cause-and-effect essay that deals with drug abuse. You can use the resources in this book for information about issues relating to drug abuse and how to structure a cause-and-effect essay. The following steps are suggestions on how to get started.

Step One: Choose your topic.

The first step is to decide what topic to write your cause-and-effect essay on. Is there any subject that particularly fascinates you? Is there an issue you strongly support, or feel strongly against? Is there a topic you feel personally connected to? Ask yourself such questions before selecting your essay topic. Refer to Appendix D: Sample Essay Topics if you need help selecting a topic.

Step Two: Write down questions and answers about the topic.

Before you begin writing, you will need to think carefully about what ideas your essay will contain. This is a process known as brainstorming. *Brainstorming* involves asking yourself questions and coming up with ideas to discuss in your essay. Possible questions that will help you with the brainstorming process include:

- Why is this topic important?
- Why should people be interested in this topic?
- How can I make this essay interesting to the reader?
- What question am I going to address in this paragraph or essay?
- What facts, ideas, or quotes can I use to support the answer to my question?

Questions especially for cause-and-effect essays include:

- What are the causes of the topic being examined?
- What are the effects of the topic being examined?
- Are there single or multiple causes?
- Are there single or multiple effects?
- Is a chain reaction or domino series of events involved?

Step Three: Gather facts, ideas, and anecdotes related to your topic.

This book contains several places to find information, including the viewpoints and the appendices. In addition, you may want to research the books, articles, and Web sites listed in Section III, or do additional research in your local library. You can also conduct interviews if you know someone who has a compelling story that would fit well in your essay.

Step Four: Develop a workable thesis statement.

Use what you have written down in steps two and three to help you articulate the main point or argument you want to make in your essay. It should be expressed in a clear sentence and make an arguable or supportable point.

Example:

The government has wrongly opposed legalizing marijuana for medical purposes; several convincing studies show that marijuana can be an effective medicine for the right patient.

This could be the thesis statement of a multiple effects essay that argues in favor of legalizing medicinal marijuana.

Step Five: Write an outline or diagram.

1. Write the thesis statement at the top of the outline.
2. Write roman numerals I, II, and III on the left side of the page.
3. Next to each Roman numeral, write down the best ideas you came up with in step three. These should all directly relate to and support the thesis statement.

4. Next to each letter write down information that supports that particular idea.

Step Six: Write the three supporting paragraphs.

Use your outline to write the three supporting paragraphs. Write down the main idea of each paragraph in sentence form. Do the same thing for the supporting points of information. Each sentence should support the paragraph of the topic. Be sure you have relevant and interesting details, facts, and quotes. Use transitions when you move from idea to idea to keep the text fluid and smooth. Sometimes, although not always, paragraphs can include a concluding or summary sentence that restates the paragraph's argument.

Step Seven: Write the introduction and conclusion.

See Exercise 3A for information on writing introductions and conclusions.

Step Eight: Read and rewrite.

As you read, check your essay for the following:

- ✔ Does the essay maintain a consistent tone?
- ✔ Do all paragraphs reinforce your general thesis?
- ✔ Do all paragraphs flow from one to the other? Do you need to add transition words or phrases?
- ✔ Have you quoted from reliable, authoritative, and interesting sources?
- ✔ Is there a sense of progression throughout the essay?
- ✔ Does the essay get bogged down in too much detail or irrelevant material?
- ✔ Does your introduction grab the reader's attention?
- ✔ Does your conclusion reflect back on any previously discussed material, or give the essay a sense of closure?
- ✔ Are there any spelling or grammatical errors?

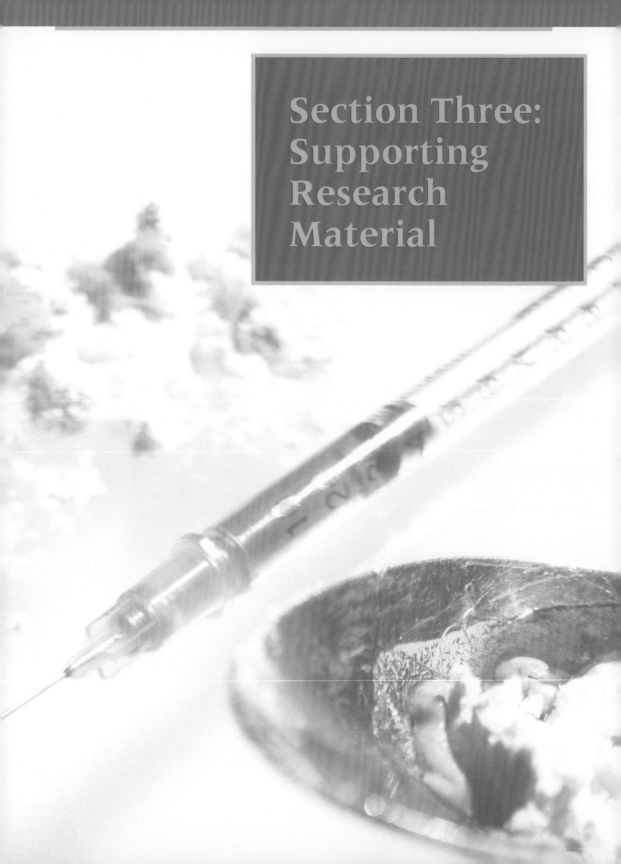

Section Three: Supporting Research Material

Facts About Drug Abuse

Editor's Note: These facts can be used in reports or papers to reinforce or add credibility when making important points or claims.

Facts about Nation-Wide Drug Use

The Office of National Drug Control Policy reports that the most commonly used illegal drugs by those over the age of 12 are:

- Marijuana—5.4% of the population or 12.1 million users;
- Cocaine—0.7% of the population or 1.7 million users;
- Hallucinogens (including LSD, PCP, and ecstasy)— 0.6% of the population or 1.3 million users.

The U.S. Substance Abuse and Mental Health Services Administration (SAMSA) reports that five substances accounted for 95 percent of all substance abuse treatment admissions in 2004:

- alcohol (40 percent)
- heroin (18 percent)
- marijuana (16 percent)
- cocaine (14 percent)
- methamphetamines (8 percent).

SAMHSA also reports that the number of people receiving treatment for methamphetamine addiction has increased four fold since 1993.

According to the National Survey on Drug Use and Health:

- In 2005, there were 2.4 million persons who were current cocaine users, up from 2004, when the number was 2.0 million.

- The number of current crack users increased from 467,000 in 2004 to 682,000 in 2005.
- Hallucinogens were used in the past month by 1.1 million persons (0.4 percent) in 2005, including 502,000 (0.2 percent) who had used Ecstasy.
- There were approximately 136,000 active heroin users in 2005.
- There were 9.0 million people aged 12 or older (3.7 percent) who were current users of illicit drugs other than marijuana in 2005. Most (6.4 million, 2.6 percent) used psychotherapeutic drugs. Of these, 4.7 million used pain relievers, 1.8 million used tranquilizers, 1.1 million used stimulants (including 512,000 using methamphetamine), and 272,000 used sedatives.
- 110 million Americans aged 12 or over (45.8% of the U.S. population aged 12 and over) report having used an illicit drug at least once in their lifetime.
- Approximately 36 million Americans have reported abusing prescription drugs at least once in their lifetime.
- Among the 16.7 million heavy drinkers in America, 32.2 % are also illicit drug users.
- An estimated 10.6 million persons reported driving under the influence of an illicit drug during the past year.
- An estimated 3.8 million people aged 12 or older (1.6 percent of the population) received some kind of treatment for a problem related to the use of alcohol or illicit drugs in 2004.
- Of these, 1.5 million received treatment for the use of both alcohol and illicit drugs and 0.7 million received treatment for the use of illicit drugs but not alcohol.
- In 2004, males were more than twice as likely as females to receive treatment for an alcohol or an illicit drug use problem in the past year.

Drug Abuse in Schools

- According to the Center for Addiction and Substance Abuse (CASA), from 2004 to 2005, the percentage of teens who know a friend or classmate who has abused prescription drugs increased 86%.
- The percentage of students who have used methamphetamine at least once has dropped from 9.1 % in 1999 to 6.2% in 2005, according to the U.S. Centers for Disease Control.
- According to the Office of National Drug Control Policy (ONDCP) there were 600,000 fewer teens using drugs in 2005 than there were in 2001.
- Studies conducted by the American Association of Clinical Chemistry, have found that the error rate in drug testing is around 3%.
- A 2003 study published in the *Journal of School Health* found that marijuana use was the same in schools that tested students for drugs as it was in schools that did not test for drugs.

According to a 2004 drug testing survey by Western Illinois University, the most commonly tested drugs in schools are

- Marijuana (tested for by 100% of drug-testing schools)
- Methamphetamines (tested for by 95% of drug testing schools)
- Opiates (tested for by 95% of drug-testing schools)
- Cocaine (tested for by 77% of drug-testing schools)
- Alcohol (tested for by 77% of drug-testing schools)
- LSD (tested for by 27% of drug-testing schools)
- Ecstasy (tested for by 18% of drug-testing schools)
- PCP (tested for by 18% of drug-testing schools)

According to the 2005 University of Michigan Monitoring the Future Survey:

- Overall drug use among 8th, 10th, and 12th graders has declined by 19% since 2001.
- Less than 10 percent of 12th graders use LSD annually.

- 45 percent of 12th graders report it would be "fairly easy" or "very easy" for them to get cocaine if they wanted.
- 30 percent of 12th-graders report they could get heroin fairly easily if they wanted.
- More school-aged boys than girls report steroid use. In 2005, annual rates of steroid use were 1.2%, 1.8%, and 2.6% for boys in grades 8, 10, and 12, compared with 0.9%, 0.7%, and 0.4% for girls.

Costs of Drug Abuse

- In 2007, President Bush asked the U.S. Congress for almost $19.6 million to spend on student drug testing in schools.
- According to drug abuse expert Meredith Maran, drug abuse costs the U.S. economy $414 billion a year.
- In 2005, the U.S. government spent approximately $12.6 billion dollars to fight drug use and abuse, including about $2 billion for stopping drug use, about $3 billion for healing drug users, and about $7.5 billion to disrupt drug supply markets.

Facts about Marijuana

- According to the United Nations Office on Drugs and Crime, marijuana is the most commonly used drug world-wide. In 2005 close to 160 million people in the world used marijuana, but only 11 million used heroin and about 14 million used cocaine.

The National Institute on Drug Abuse reports:

- Marijuana is the most commonly used illegal drug in the U.S.
- Nearly 45% of U.S. teenagers try marijuana before finishing high school.]
- Over 280,000 people entering drug treatment programs reported marijuana as their primary drug of abuse in 2002.

According to the 2004 National Survey on Drug Use and Health (NSDUH):

- Approximately 96.8 million Americans ages 12 and older (about 40.2% of the population) have reported trying marijuana at least once during their lifetimes,
- Approximately 25.5 million people (10.6% of the population) reported past year marijuana use and 14.6 million people (6.1%) reported past month marijuana use.
- 3.2 million persons use marijuana on a daily or almost-daily basis.
- The number of youths aged 12 to 17 using marijuana daily or almost daily declined from 358,000 in 2002 to 282,000 in 2003, but increased to 342,000 in 2004.
- According to the Marijuana Policy Project, in 2004 about 6,000 people a day used marijuana for the first time—2.1 million Americans.
- Students with an average grade of "D" or below were four times as likely to have used marijuana in the past year as students who reported an average grade of "A."

According to the U.S. Drug Enforcement Agency:

- Average levels of THC (the main active ingredient) in marijuana have risen from less than 1% in the mid-1970s to more than 8% in 2004.
- A 50% concentration of THC can be found in the body—particularly the testes, liver, and brain—up to eight days after using marijuana. Traces of THC can be found in the body up to 3 months after use.

According to a study reported in the *Journal of the American Medical Association,* a study of 300 sets of twins revealed that marijuana-using twins were four times more likely than their non-using siblings to use cocaine and five times more likely to use LSD.

Medical Marijuana

- As of March 2007, twelve states have medical marijuana laws that make it permissible for people with certain debilitating diseases to grow or possess marijuana or have decriminalized marijuana for such use—Alaska, Arizona, California, Colorado, Hawaii, Maine, Maryland, Nevada, Oregon, Rhode Island, Vermont and Washington.

- More than 25 health organizations have endorsed the use of marijuana for medical purposes, including: the Institute of Medicine, the American Academy of Family Physicians; American Bar Association; American Public Health Association; American Society of Addiction Medicine; AIDS Action Council; British Medical Association; California Academy of Family Physicians; California Legislative Council for Older Americans; California Medical Association; California Nurses Association; California Pharmacists Association; California Society of Addiction Medicine; California-Pacific Annual Conference of the United Methodist Church; Colorado Nurses Association; *Consumer Reports Magazine;* Kaiser Permanente; Lymphoma Foundation of America; Multiple Sclerosis California Action Network; National Association of Attorneys General; National Association of People with AIDS; National Nurses Society on Addictions; New Mexico Nurses Association; New York State Nurses Association; New England Journal of Medicine; and the Virginia Nurses Association.A survey of Californians reports the top three reported uses of medicinal marijuana were for chronic pain (40%), AIDS-related (22%) and mood disorders (15%).

- According to an October 2002 *Time Magazine/CNN Poll*, 80 percent of respondents supported allowing adults to "legally use marijuana for medical purposes."

- A November 2004 poll conducted by the AARP (American Association of Retired Persons), found that 72 percent of respondents agreed with the statement, "Adults should be allowed to legally use marijuana for medical purposes if a physician recommends it."

According to the National Organization for the Reform of Marijuana Laws (NORML):

- No one has ever died from an overdose of marijuana.
- Marijuana can treat a wide range of disorders and medical problems, including chronic pain, nausea, spasticity, glaucoma, movement disorders, wasting disorders, and dementia.
- A *Journal of Neuroscience* study showed that chemicals found naturally in marijuana called cannabinoids can reduce inflammation in the brain and may protect it from the cognitive decline associated with Alzheimer's disease.

Finding and Using Sources of Information

No matter what type of essay you are writing, it is necessary to find information to support your point of view. You can use sources such as books, magazine articles, newspaper articles, and online articles.

Using Books and Articles

You can find books and articles in a library by using the library's computer or cataloging system. If you are not sure how to use these resources, ask a librarian to help you. You can also use a computer to find many magazine articles and other articles written specifically for the Internet.

You are likely to find a lot more information than you can possibly use in your essay, so your first task is to narrow it down to what is likely to be most usable. Look at book and article titles. Look at book chapter titles, and examine the book's index to see if it contains information on the specific topic you want to write about. (For example, if you want to write about the efficacy of the War on Drugs and you find a book about marijuana use, check the chapter titles and index to be sure it contains information about the War on Drugs before you bother to check out the book.)

For a five-paragraph essay, you do not need a great deal of supporting information, so quickly try to narrow down your materials to a few good books and magazine or Internet articles. You do not need dozens. You might even find that one or two good books or articles contain all the information you need.

You probably do not have time to read an entire book, so find the chapters or sections that relate to your topic, and skim these. When you find useful information, copy it onto a note card or notebook. You should look for supporting facts, statistics, quotations, and examples.

Using the Internet

When you select your supporting information, it is important that you evaluate its source. This is especially important with information you find on the Internet. Because nearly anyone can put information on the Internet, there is as much bad information as good information. Before using Internet information—or any information—try to determine if the source seems to be reliable. Is the author or Internet site sponsored by a legitimate organization? Is it from a government source? Does the author have any special knowledge or training relating to the topic you are looking up? Does the article give any indication of where its information comes from?

Using Your Supporting Information

When you use supporting information from a book, article, interview or other source, there are three important things to remember:

1. *Make it clear whether you are using a direct quotation or a paraphrase.* If you copy information directly from your source, you are quoting it. You must put quotation marks around the information, and tell where the information comes from. If you put the information in your own words, you are paraphrasing it.

    Here is an example of a using a quotation:
    Author Diana Mahoney believes that the heavy pressure put on student athletes forces them to turn to performance-enhancing drugs, such as steroids. "They're taking them to get strong, to get lean, to get validation, and to get scholarships—and they're doing it under the noses of their parents, coaches, and teachers." (50).

Here is an example of a brief paraphrase of the same passage:

> Author Diana Mahoney believes that the heavy pressure put on student athletes forces them to turn to performance-enhancing drugs, such as steroids. She argues that teens turn to these drugs in order to build up their strength, trim fat, feel good about themselves, and to qualify for athletic scholarships that could be their ticket to college. Worse, says Mahoney, they are doing it under the very watch of the people who tend to put this pressure on them—their parents, coaches, and teachers.

2. *Use the information fairly.* Be careful to use supporting information in the way the author intended it. For example, it is unfair to quote an author as saying, "The War on Drugs has been an overwhelming success" when he or she intended to say, "The War on Drugs has been an overwhelming success—on increasing drug use, reducing civil liberties, and instituting a decades-long propaganda program." This is called taking information out of context. This practice uses supporting evidence unfairly.

3. *Give credit where credit is due.* Giving credit is known as citing. You must use citations when you use someone else's information, but not every piece of supporting information needs a citation.

   - If the supporting information is general knowledge—that is, it can be found in many sources—you do not have to cite your source.
   - If you directly quote a source, you must cite it.
   - If you paraphrase information from a specific source, you must cite it. If you do not use citations where you should, you are *plagiarizing*—or stealing—someone else's work.

Citing Your Sources

There are a number of ways to cite your sources. Your teacher will probably want you to do it in one of three ways:

- Informal: As in the example in number 1 above, tell where you got the information as you present it in the text of your essay.
- Informal list: At the end of your essay, place an unnumbered list of all the sources you used. This tells the reader where, in general, your information came from
- Formal: Use numbered footnotes. Footnotes are generally placed at the end of an article or essay, although they may be placed elsewhere depending on your teacher's requirements.

Works Cited

Mahoney, Diana. "Teens and Steroids: a Dangerous Mix." *Clinical Psychiatry News* June 2006: 50.

Using MLA Style to Create a Works Cited List

You will probably need to create a list of works cited for your paper. These include materials that you quoted from, relied heavily on, or consulted to write your paper. There are several different ways to structure these references. The following examples are based on Modern Language Association (MLA) style, one of the major citation styles used by writers.

Book Entries

For most book entries you will need the author's name, the book's title, where it was published, what company published it, and the year it was published. This information is usually found on the inside of the book. Variations on book entries include the following:

A book by a single author:
> Guest, Emma. *Children of AIDS: Africa's Orphan Crisis.* London: Sterling, 2003.

Two or more books by the same author:
> Friedman, Thomas L. *The World Is Flat: A Brief History of the Twentieth Century.* New York: Farrar, Straus and Giroux, 2005.
>
> ---. *From Beirut to Jerusalem.* New York: Doubleday, 1989.

A book by two or more authors:
> Pojman, Louis P., and Jeffrey Reiman. *The Death Penalty: For and Against.* Lanham, MD: Rowman & Littlefield, 1998.

A book with an editor:
> Friedman, Lauri S., ed. *At Issue: What Motivates Suicide Bombers?* San Diego, CA: Greenhaven, 2004.

Periodical and Newspaper Entries

Entries for sources found in periodicals and newspapers are cited a bit differently than books. For one, these sources usually have a title and a publication name. They also may have specific dates and page numbers. Unlike book entries, you do not need to list where newspapers or periodicals are published or what company publishes them.

An Article from a Periodical:
> Snow, Keith Harmon. "State Terror in Ethiopia." *Z Magazine* June 2004: 33–35.

An Unsigned Article from a Periodical:
> "Broadcast Decency Rules." *Issues & Controversies on File* 30 Apr. 2004.

An Article from a Newspaper:
> Constantino, Rebecca. "Fostering Love, Respecting Race." *Los Angeles Times* 14 Dec. 2002: B17.

Internet Sources

To document a source you found online, try to provide as much information on it as possible, including the author's name, the title of the document, date of publication or of last revision, the URL, and your date of access.

A Web Source:
> Shyovitz, David. "The History and Development of Yiddish." Jewish Virtual Library. 30 May 2005 http://www.jewishvirtuallibrary.org/jsource/History/yiddish.html. Accessed September 11, 2007.

Your teacher will tell you exactly how information should be cited in your essay. Generally, the very least information needed is the original author's name and the name of the article or other publication.

Be sure you know exactly what information your teacher requires before you start looking for your supporting information so that you know what information to include with your notes.

Sample Essay Topics

Drug Abuse Is a Serious Problem
Drug Abuse Is Not a Serious Problem
Teen Drug Abuse Is a Serious Problem
Teen Drug Abuse Is Not a Serious Problem
Examining the Causes of Drug Abuse
Examining the Effects of Drug Abuse

The War on Drugs Reduces Drug Abuse
The War on Drugs Does not Reduce Drug Abuse
Legalizing Drugs Would Reduce Drug Abuse
Legalizing Drugs Would Increase Drug Abuse
Student Drug Testing Reduces Drug Abuse
Student Drug Testing Does Not Reduce Drug Abuse

Marijuana Is a Gateway to the Use of Harder Drugs
Marijuana Is Not a Gateway to the Use of Harder Drugs
Medicinal Marijuana Should Be Legal
Medicinal Marijuana Should Not Be Legal
The Benefits of Medical Marijuana
The Dangers of Medical Marijuana
The Health Effects of Marijuana
The Impact of Marijuana on America's Youth
States Should Legalize Medical Marijuana
States Should Not Legalize Medical Marijuana

Organizations to Contact

American Civil Liberties Union (ACLU)
125 Broad St., 18th Fl., New York, NY 10004-2400 •
(212) 549-2500 • e-mail: aclu@aclu.org • Web site:
http://www.aclu.org

The ACLU is a national organization that works to defend
Americans' civil rights guaranteed by the U.S. Constitution.
It provides legal defense, research, and education. The
ACLU opposes the criminal prohibition of marijuana and
the civil liberties violations that result from it.

American Council for Drug Education (ACDE)
164 W. 74th St., New York, NY 10023 • (800) 488-DRUG
• e-mail: acde@phoenixhouse.org • Web site: http://
www.acde.org

The American Council for Drug Education informs the
public about the harmful effects of abusing drugs and
alcohol. It gives the public access to scientifically based,
compelling prevention programs and materials.

Cato Institute
1000 Massachusetts Ave., NW, Washington, DC
20001-5403 • (202) 842-0200 • e-mail: service@cato.
org • Web site: http://www.cato.org

The institute is a public policy research foundation dedicated to limiting the control of government and to protect-
ing individual liberty. Cato, which strongly favors drug
legalization, publishes the *Cato Journal* three times a year
and the *Cato Policy Report* bimonthly.

Drug Enforcement Administration (DEA)

2401 Jefferson Davis Highway, Alexandria, VA 22301 •
(202) 307-1000 • Web site: http://www.dea.gov

The DEA is the federal agency charged with enforcing the nation's drug laws. The agency concentrates on stopping the smuggling and distribution of narcotics in the United States and abroad. It publishes the *Drug Enforcement Magazine* three times a year.

The Drug Policy Alliance

70 West 36th Street, 16th Floor New York, NY 10018 •
(212) 613-8020 • e-mail: dc@drugpolicy.org • Web site:
http://www.dpf.org/homepage.cfm

The Drug Policy Alliance is the leading organization in the United States promoting alternatives to the war on drugs. The Alliance supports the creation of drug policies that respect individual rights, protect community health, and minimize the involvement of the criminal justice system

The Drug Reform Coordination Network

1623 Connecticut Ave., NW, 3rd Floor Washington, DC 20009 • (202) 293-8340 • e-mail: drcnet@drcnet.org •
Web site: http://stopthedrugwar.org

The Drug Reform Coordination Network opposes the "War on Drugs" and works for drug policy reform from a variety of perspectives, including harm reduction, reform of sentencing and forfeiture laws, medicalization of marijuana, and the promotion of an open debate on drug prohibition.

Join Together

One Appleton Street 4th floor Boston, MA 02116-5223 •
(617) 437-1500 • e-mail: info@jointogether.org • Web site: http://www.jointogether.org

Founded in 1991, Join Together supports community-based efforts to reduce, prevent, and treat substance abuse. It publishes community action kits to facilitate grassroots efforts to increase awareness of substance abuse issues as well as a quarterly newsletter.

Marijuana Policy Project

PO Box 77492-Capitol Hill, Washington, DC 20013 • (202) 462-5747 • e-mail: mpp@mpp.org • Web site: http://www.mpp.org

The Marijuana Policy Project develops and promotes policies to minimize the harm associated with marijuana. It is the only organization that is solely concerned with lobbying to reform the marijuana laws on the federal level.

Multidisciplinary Association for Psychedelic Studies (MAPS)

10424 Love Creek Road, Ben Lomond, CA 95005 • (831) 336- 4325 • e-mail: askmaps@maps.org • Web site: http://www.maps.org

MAPS is a membership-based research and educational organization. It focuses on the development of beneficial, socially sanctioned uses of psychedelic drugs and marijuana. MAPS helps scientific researchers obtain governmental approval for funding on psychedelic research on human volunteers.

National Center on Addiction and Substance Abuse at Columbia University (CASA)

633 Third Avenue, 19th Floor New York, NY 10017-6706 • (212) 841-5200 • Web site: http://www. casacolumbia.org

CASA is a private nonprofit organization that works to educate the public about the costs and hazards of substance abuse and the prevention and treatment of all forms of chemical dependency. The center supports treatment as the best way to reduce drug addiction.

National Clearinghouse for Alcohol and Drug Information

PO Box 2345, Rockville, MD 20847-2345 •
(800) 729-6686 • e-mail: shs@health.org • Web site:
http://www.health.org

The clearinghouse distributes publications of the U.S.
Department of Health and Human Services, the National
Institute on Drug Abuse, and other federal agencies
concerned with alcohol and drug abuse. Brochure titles
include *Tips for Teens About Marijuana*.

National Institute on Drug Abuse (NIDA)

6001 Executive Blvd. Rm. 5213 MSC 9561, Bethesda, MD
20892-9561 • (301) 443-6245 • e-mail: information@
nida.nih.gov • Web site: http://www.nida.nih.gov

NIDA supports and conducts research on drug abuse—
including the yearly *Monitoring the Future Survey*—to
improve addiction prevention, treatment, and policy
efforts. It publishes the bimonthly *NIDA Notes* newsletter, the periodic *NIDA Capsules* fact sheets, and a catalog
of research reports and public education materials, such
as *Marijuana: Facts for Teens and Marijuana: Facts Parents
Need to Know*.

National Organization for the Reform of Marijuana Laws (NORML)

1600 K Street, NW Washington, DC, 20006 •
202-483-5500 • e-mail: norml@norml.org • Web site:
www.normal.org

NORML fights to legalize marijuana and to help those
who have been convicted and sentenced for possessing or
selling marijuana. In addition to pamphlets and position
papers, it publishes the newsletter *Marijuana Highpoints*,
the bimonthly *Legislative Bulletin* and *Freedom@NORML*,
and the monthly Potpourri.

Office of National Drug Control Policy (ONDCP)

PO Box 6000, Rockville, MD 20849-6000 • (800) 666–3332 • e-mail: ondcp@ncjrs.org • Web site: http://www.whitehousedrugpolicy.gov

The Office of National Drug Control Policy is responsible for formulating the government's national drug strategy and the president's anti-drug policy as well as coordinating the federal agencies responsible for stopping drug trafficking. Drug policy studies are available upon request.

Partnership for a Drug-Free America

405 Lexington Ave., Suite 1601, New York, NY 10174 • (212) 922-1560 • Web site: http://www.drugfreeamerica.org

The Partnership for a Drug-Free America is a nonprofit organization that utilizes media communication to reduce demand for illicit drugs in America. Best known for its national antidrug advertising campaign, the partnership works to "unsell" drugs to children and to prevent drug use among kids.

Bibliography

Books

Booth, Martin, *Cannabis: A History.* New York: Doubleday, 2003. A history of marijuana use and prohibition.

Earleywine, Mitchell, *Understanding Marijuana: A New Look at the Scientific Evidence.* New York: Oxford University Press, 2002.

Fish, Jefferson M., ed., *Drugs and Society: U.S. Public Policy.* Lanham, MD: Rowman & Littlefield, 2006.

Fitzhugh, Karla, *Prescription Drug Abuse,* Chicago, IL: Heinemann Library, 2006.

Huggins, Laura E., ed, *Drug War Deadlock: The Policy Battle Continues.* Stanford, CA: Hoover Institute, 2005.

Langwith, Jacqueline, ed., *Introducing Issues with Opposing Viewpoints: Drug Abuse.* Farmington Hills, MI: Greenhaven, 2006.

Maran, Meredith, *Dirty.* San Francisco: HarperSanFrancisco, 2003.

Rebman, Renee, *Addictions and Risky Behaviors: Cutting, Bingeing, Snorting, and Other Dangers.* Berkeley Heights, NJ: Enslow, 2006.

Rees, Jonathan, *Drugs.* North Mankato, MN: Smart Apple Media, 2006.

Periodicals

"Non-Medical Marijuana II: Rite of Passage or Russian Roulette?" National Center on Addiction and Substance Abuse, April 2004. www.casacolumbia.org/pdshop-prov/files/Marijuana_Paper_on_Letterhead.pdfwww.casacolumbia.org/pdshopprov/files/Marijuana_Paper_on_Letterhead.pdf

Barthwell, Andrea, "A Haze of Misinformation Clouds Issue of Medical Marijuana," *Los Angeles Times,* July 22, 2003.

Califano Jr., Joseph, "Accompanying Statement for Under the Counter: The Diversion and Abuse of Controlled Prescription Drugs in the U.S.," National Center on Substance Abuse and Addiction at Columbia University, July 2005.

Caulkins, Jonathon P., Peter Reuter, Martin Y. Iguchi, and James Chiesa, "How Goes the 'War on Drugs'? An Assessment of U.S. Drug Problems and Policy," *Rand Drug Policy Research Center,* 2005.

Chapman, Steve, "The Latest Drug Crisis, Again," *Chicago Tribune,* August 7, 2005.

Childress, Sarah, "My Mother the Narc," *Newsweek,* April 10, 2006.

Cohen, Harold E., "A Closer Look at Marijuana," *Drug Topics,* December 8, 2003.

Cole, Jack, "End Prohibition Now!" *Law Enforcement Against Prohibition,* September 21, 2005. www.leap.cc/publications/endprohnow.htm

Conant, Marcus, "Medical Marijuana," *Family Practice News,* July 1, 2005.

Cronkite, Walter, "Telling the Truth About the War on Drugs," *Huffington Post,* March 1, 2006.

Curley, Bob, "Treatment No Panacea for Nation's Drug Problems," *Join Together Online,* April 28, 2006.

Fay, Clavina L., "Student Drug Testing Is Part of the Solution," *Behavioral Health Management,* July–August 2004.

Friedman, Milton, "Weed All About It; Yes I think We Should Legalize Marijuana," *Texas Monthly,* July 2005.

Friedman, R. A., "The Changing Face of Teenage Drug Abuse—the Trend Toward Prescription Drugs," *New England Journal of Medicine,* April 6, 2006.

Gregory, Anthony, "The Drug War's Immorality and Abject Failure," *Future of Freedom Foundation*, October 6, 2006.

Kern, Jennifer, Fatema Gunja, Alexandra Cox, Marsha Rosenbaum, Judith Appel, and Anjuli Verna, "Making Sense of Student Drug Testing: Why Educators Are Saying No," *Drug Policy Alliance*, January 2006.

Leinwand, Donna, "Drugmakers Take Action to Foil Meth Cooks," *USA Today*, June 29, 2005.

Leverenz, Nikos A., "Testing the Wrong Policy on Students," *Brainwash*, September 19, 2004.

Maich, Steve, "A Case for Marijuana, Inc.," *Maclean's*, Vol. 117, no. 47, November 22, 2004.

Miller, Sara B., "Steps Toward More Drug Testing in Schools," *Christian Science Monitor*, May 20, 2005.

Nadelman, Ethan, "An End to Marijuana Prohibition: The Drive to Legalize Picks Up," *National Review*, 2004.

New York Times, "When Medical Marijuana is Misused," June 24, 2005.

Office of National Drug Control Policy, "Marijuana," Drug Facts, February 27, 2006.

Ribeiro, Michele Lee, Sarah Richards, "When Prescription Drugs Kill," *CosmoGirl!*, March 7, 2005.

Satel, Sally, "Much Ado About Meth?" *TCS Daily*, November 4, 2005.

Stamper, Norm, "Let Those Dopers Be," *Los Angeles Times*, October 16, 2005.

Szalavitz, Maia, "The New Reefer Madness," *Chicago Sun-Times*, October 2, 2005.

Tierney, John, "Marijuana Pipe Dreams," *New York Times*, August 27, 2005.

Walters, John P., "No Surrender: The Drug War Saves Lives," *National Review*, September 27, 2004.

U.S. Drug Enforcement Agency, "Speaking Out Against Drug Legalization," March 2003.

Web Sites

Drug War Facts (www.drugwarfacts.org). Provides facts and statistics about marijuana and marijuana laws, arguing that marijuana policies should be reformed.

Drug Watch International (www.drugwatch.org). A non-profit drug information organization that opposes the legalization of drugs and promotes the creation of drug-free cultures.

The Facts About Marijuana (www.marijuana-info.org). A Web site of the National Institute on Drug Abuse (NIDA) that provides fact sheets, reports, and articles that argue that marijuana is a dangerous drug.

Harm Reduction Journal (www.harmreductionjournal.com). An online journal that focuses on reducing the adverse medical and social consequences of drug abuse.

Just Think Twice (www.justthinktwice.com). A Web site for teens sponsored by the U.S. Drug Enforcement Administration that seeks to help teens make smart choices about drug use.

Marijuana.com (www.marijuana.com). A comprehensive source of information on the medicinal and recreational use of marijuana. Web site contains fact sheets, articles, and reports that are in favor of medical marijuana.

Index

California Medical
Association, 86
California Nurses
Association, 86
California Pharmacists
Association, 86
California Society of
Addiction Medicine, 86
California-Pacific
Annual Conference of
the United Methodist
Church, 86
Cancer, 33, 36, 52–53,
63
Cannabinoid receptors,
34
Cannabis sativa. *See*
Marijuana
Carcinogens, 36
Career status, 40
Cato Institute, 96
Cause and effect essays,
52–55, 68, 77–78
Center for Addiction
and Substance Abuse
(CASA), 83
Center for Epidemiologic
Studies Depression, 42
Centers for Disease
Control (CDC), 83
Children, 20
Chronic pain, 86–87
Civilization, 25
Clergy, 29

Cocaine, 27, 31, 64,
69–71, 81, 83
Cognitive abilities, 40
College and university,
5, 39
Colorado, 86
Colorado Nurses
Association, 86
Columbia University, 70
Conclusion, 51, 61, 67,
75, 79
Consequences, 62–64
*Consumer Reports
Magazine*, 86
Counselors, 9, 29
Crime, 18–23, 63
Crips, 22
Culture, 5
*Current Opinion in
Pharmacology*, 44

DanceSafe, 7
Dementia, 87
Depression, 37, 42–45,
58, 70
Disease, 37, 62–63, 87
Dopamine, 35
Drug Abuse Warning
Network (DAWN), 64
Drug Enforcement
Administration (DEA),
97
Drug Policy Alliance, 97

Picture Credits

About the Editor

Lauri S. Friedman earned her bachelor's degree in religion and political science from Vassar College in Poughkeepsie, NY. Her studies there focused on political Islam. Friedman has worked as a non-fiction writer, a newspaper journalist, and an editor for more than 7 years. She has accumulated extensive experience in both academic and professional settings.

Friedman has edited and authored numerous publications for Greenhaven Press on controversial social issues such as gay marriage, Islam, energy, discrimination, suicide bombers, and the war on terror. Much of the *Writing the Critical Essay* series has been under her direction or authorship. She was instrumental in the creation of the series, and played a critical role in its conception and development.